WILLS & TRUSTS

A LEGAL AND FINANCIAL HANDBOOK FOR EVERYONE

CHARLES F. HEMPHILL, Jr.
M.S., Doctor of Jurisprudence
Member of the Texas Bar

Edited by
Phyllis Davis Hemphill
Rio Hondo College

A SPECTRUM BOOK

Prentice-Hall, Inc., Englewood Cliffs, N.J.

Library of Congress Cataloging in Publication Data

Hemphill, Charles F
  Wills & trusts.

  (Spectrum Book)
  Includes index.
  1. Estate planning—United States. 2. Wills—United
States. 3. Trusts and trustees—United States.
4. Tax planning—United States. I. Hemphill,
Phyllis D., 1919–   II. Title.
KF750.H39   346'.73'052   79-22182
ISBN 0-13-960237-2
ISBN 0-13-960229-1 pbk.

This publication is designed to provide accurate and authoritative information in regard to the subject matter covered. It is sold with the understanding that the publisher is not engaged in rendering legal, accounting or other professional service. If legal advice or other expert assistance is required, the services of a competent professional person should be sought.—*From a Declaration of Principles jointly adopted by a Committee of the American Bar Association and a Committee of Publishers.*

A SPECTRUM BOOK

10 9 8 7 6 5 4 3 2 1

Printed in the United States of America

PRENTICE-HALL INTERNATIONAL, INC., *London*
PRENTICE-HALL OF AUSTRALIA PTY. LIMITED, *Sydney*
PRENTICE-HALL OF CANADA, LTD., *Toronto*
PRENTICE-HALL OF INDIA PRIVATE LIMITED, *New Delhi*
PRENTICE-HALL OF JAPAN, INC., *Tokyo*
PRENTICE-HALL OF SOUTHEAST ASIA PTE. LTD., *Singapore*
WHITEHALL BOOKS LIMITED, WELLINGTON, *New Zealand*

Contents

4

Disinheritance: Bequests to Other Than Ordinary Heirs   36

5

Some Other Types of Wills   51

6

Getting Your Will Written   57

Writing Your Own Will   69

7

Other Provisions That May Be Included In Your Will 73

8

Rewriting Your Will 81

9

Probate 88

II

Taxation And Property Accumulation: Saving on Gift And Estate Taxes   99

13

The Federal Gift Tax   138

14

Charitable Bequests As Tax Deductions   147

III

Trusts As Tools in Estate Planning   151

15

Trusts—Their Nature and Makeup   153

Preface

This is a book to help you stretch the dollars that you are accumulating. It is about people and money problems, and how these problems may be solved to advantage.

We are all concerned with protecting our property—concerned both for ourselves and for those who may eventually receive property from us.

This is also a book about law, but it is not a book for lawyers. It is to inform you of the number and possibility of choices open to every person who wants to accumulate money or property, and to pass on this accumulation to those you want to benefit from it. Written in non-technical language, insofar as possible, this book is designed to give you a working background for planning your own estate and your will.

This was not prepared as a text on estate planning, in the technical sense. A lawyer or tax specialist in that field would need far more than can be obtained from a volume of this kind. Rather, this is a little book to lay out guideposts for those estate problems that may eventually face you and members of your own immediate family. Without a basic understanding of wills and trusts laws, estate problems may be costly, both in emotional and financial terms.

Wills and trusts are among the legal tools most commonly used to control where your property goes. It is almost always preferable to use such legal tools, rather than to have your property distributed according to the arbitrary plan set up by state inheritance laws (laws of devise and descent).

Besides allowing you to designate who is to receive your property, wills and trusts may help you avoid unnecessary costs, charges, and taxes.

This book is not a do-it-yourself manual to train you as your own lawyer or tax consultant, or to set up your own trust. Frankly, no book should be relied upon to take the place of an attorney in certain matters. However, most adults are capable of writing a legal will. And while a do-it-yourself publication would be useful in some instances, at other times, trying to use a manual instead of consulting an attorney can cause a great deal of harm.

This book is designed to help you decide when you need legal assistance—to avoid some of the problems that fall on those who do not have a working knowledge of laws and legal customs.

In addition, this book should help those many individuals who may be called upon to serve as an executor or executrix for a relative or friend.

The term *spouse* is used with considerable frequency, to mean the legally married mate of a man or woman. *Spouse* does not refer to individuals living together without marriage.

Matters relating to estate and trust problems vary from jurisdiction to jurisdiction. In some states these matters are handled in a Circuit Court, in others a County Court, a District Court, a Superior Court, a Chancery Court, or a Law and Equity Court.

Taxation laws are subject to frequent change. And the tax laws of every state are unique to that jurisdiction. In general, the tax laws that concern us here, however, are the Federal estate tax, the Federal gift tax, and the Federal income tax laws, that are applied uniformly in all states. But there are so many adjustments, refinements, and exceptions to all tax laws that it is seldom possible to give absolute answers. Yet an understanding of general legal principles will aid in handling your own estate.

While not designed as a text, this book includes a few footnotes of legal case citations with unusual interest. If you have access to a law library, these cases may be worth reading.

I want to express appreciation to Carol Chase of the California Bar, and to Mrs. Margaret Morse for manuscript preparation.

It is hoped that this book will point the way to greater enjoyment of that which is yours, and in retaining better control of your money and assets.

CHARLES F. HEMPHILL, JR.

Long Beach, California

I

What a Will Is, And How It May Serve Your Best Interests

1

The Advantages in Accumulating, Using, And Leaving Money by Will

We all want to control and enjoy our property, and we want to make good use of it all through our lives. Few people can afford to risk giving away a large part of their property or money before death, nor can they afford to. But eventually we expect to decide how it will be passed on and to avoid having it eaten away by unnecessary court costs, charges, and taxes.

AN ESTATE FOR EVERYONE

If you have personal belongings—possessions or property of any kind—you have an estate. An *estate* is the sum total of all you own or have a financial interest in, over and above the debts that you owe.

But "estate" is a rich sounding word. A common misconception about an estate is that one must be rich to be classified as an estate holder. The average adult owns a car, equity in a house or other real estate, a life insurance policy, a vested interest in a company pension and/or Social Security benefits, a portion of a business, credit union shares, or some other investments.

Today, you may have a tendency to overlook some of your assets and to downplay their eventual worth. In the future, within a decade or two, your estate may be far larger and more involved than you now realize.

HAVING OVERALL
ESTATE OBJECTIVES

It follows that anyone who has possessions or property may need a well organized estate management plan.

There is usually more to estate planning than selecting a method to dispose of one's money and assets. Almost anyone can get rid of what he or she owns with little difficulty. The question is whether the method of disposal will give reasonable assurance that the bequest will be used to best advantage, viewed from the wishes of the original owner as well as of those intended to receive the property.

Wills and trusts are usually a vital part of estate management. Of the tools and legal devices used in estate planning, a will is probably the most familiar. While a will is not the only tool that may be used, it is one of the basics.

As life grows increasingly complex, it is difficult to disassociate estate planning from life planning. Many of the things one does during the ordinary affairs of life affect one's estate. The estate plan must suit the family or business situation which it will in fact control. The approach taken may depend on the family, but in many instances estate planning for married people should be a project for both husband and wife. There are times when it may be desirable to also bring older children into the planning.

BASIC OBJECTIVES
OF AN ESTATE PLAN

In considering your own estate plan, you may be surprised to see the real extent of your worth. This worth may be estimated by drawing up an evaluation of your assets by using the form in Appendix 1, at the end of the book.

The basic objectives of an estate plan usually include the following:

1. protecting and conserving your financial resources, to make them available for your own wants and for those of others you may desire to assist;

2. working out the transfer of property or money, both before and after death, to recipients you desire; and

3. minimizing the tax load, charges, and court costs for you and your beneficiaries.

A good estate plan utilizes written legal instruments that clearly indicate how you want your property handled, along with the legal authority to get this done. While we normally think of a will as the most useful of these legal devices, there are other devices that may be equally helpful. These legal tools, which will be discussed later, include the following:

1. a will,

2. joint or survivorship arrangements of property ownership,

3. life insurance,

4. lifetime and testamentary trusts and

5. a power of appointment.

There are times when even a highly successful business person asks, "What do I need with an estate plan? I have an expanding, growing business, which my wife and kids will get when I die." This is one of the individuals for whom a specific plan may be especially important. It is time for every individual to speculate about how the business will be carried on, and what the family can realize from it when the business owner is no longer at the helm of the enterprise. Where can the heirs obtain enough cash to pay estate taxes, and how may family control of the business be continued?

Today, many women find themselves the major support of a family. Consequently, estate planning is important in the financial planning of those women who try to assure the best possible future for herself and those dependent on her.

In a closely knit family, estate planning can be an affair for all members who are mature enough to accept responsibility; it is best not to postpone it to a "suitable time." For most of us, the time is now.

SETTING UP YOUR INDIVIDUAL ESTATE OBJECTIVES

Without thinking the problem through, some say that everyone has the same basic objectives—simply to accumulate and to pass on money or property. While this assumption is a good generalization, it does not consider the specifics that must be settled in any estate plan. Who should get the maximum benefit of your accumulation? Should it be your wife, your children, your grandchildren, a charity, or friends?

A husband may want to leave as large an estate as possible to his wife, taking it for granted that their children will then receive whatever is not used up by the wife. But if the objective is for the husband and wife to pass on the maximum amount of property to their children, they may need a different estate plan that makes use of one or more trusts, or some other legal tools. Under this latter plan, it is intended that the surviving wife would be well cared for. But under such a plan, she might not actually receive outright ownership of some of the husband's assets such as stocks and bonds, from which she would derive income.

Since there would be different federal estate tax liabilities under these two plans, a larger sum might eventually be passed on to the couple's children by the second plan. (We will get into more detail on this later.) On the other hand, this second estate plan might not be appropriate if the estate turned out to be relatively modest and if there should be any question about the widow's financial needs during her life.

In any event, family considerations and needs must come before other matters in estate planning. Preparation should not be put off until you decide to retire—homework should start when you first begin to accumulate, or when you begin to scheme for the future.

With some exceptions, almost every adult needs a will. There is more to making up a will, however, than simply deciding whether you need one. Make sure a will is properly drawn because many a family has been torn apart by one improperly drawn.

THE WILL AS A MAJOR TOOL IN AN ESTATE PLAN

Your Legal Right To Make a Will

Almost all nations that have attained some degree of civilization have recognized the right to private ownership of property. And property owners in most of these nations have had some voice about the disposition of property after death. There are references to written wills far back in history, but it is doubtful whether ordinary individuals were allowed to use them the way we do today. Now only barely legible, the terms of a will written by Nek'ure, son of the Egyptian Pharaoh Khafre, about 2601 B.C., were carved on the wall of his tomb. In his will, which states that he was in good health and sound mind, Nek'ure disposed of 14 towns and two other estates he owned. Another ancient Egyptian will was that of Uah, written on papyrus around 1799 B.C., unearthed in 1905 A.D. by a British Egyptologist and translated by an Oxford scholar.

A famous will that has survived in its original form was that of the famous Assyrian monarch Sennacherib, written on baked clay tablets (brick) sometime before 681 B.C. Sennacherib's will disposed of jeweled bracelets, coronets, objects of gold, ivory, and precious stones that were stored in a temple for safekeeping. Old Testament references indicate that oral wills may have been used, along with written wills. The law of the ancient Babylonian King Hammurabi, written around 1950 B.C., sets out the right to dispose of property by a will. During the Roman Empire, nobles were allowed to write wills, leaving them with the keepers of the temples for safekeeping, but it is doubtful that common people had this right.

In the United States, almost all our legal background comes from the English law. Up to the time of King Henry VIII of England (about 1500), all land was owned by the king or the church. When the landholder died, the property reverted to the feudal lord or to the king himself. Only since 1541 A.D. have private individuals in England had the right to leave land or real estate by will. This right was a part of our legal heritage that the American colonists brought to the new world.[1]

The only right that an American has to dispose of property after death is that set up by legislative authority in the individual

---

[1]Girard Trust Company v. Schmitz, 20 A. 2d 21.

states. There is no authority to do so granted in the United States Constitution or in any of our other basic sources of law. As stated by the courts, the right to dispose of one's property by will has never been regarded as one of the so-called "natural rights" of humankind; it is a privilege granted by the state legislature. Theoretically, it could be taken away by the same legislature. Therefore, an owner's right to dispose of property by will is completely subject to control by the individual state government. The state we live in can withhold or place restrictions on this right as the legislature chooses.[2] People commonly have misconceptions about wills because they do not understand that laws relating to wills and estates vary from state to state. Courts have consistently ruled that a valid will must conform to the individual requirements and regulations set up by the individual state legislature.[3] This basic principle cannot be overemphasized to anyone making a will.

The Price You Pay If You Die Without a Will (Dying Intestate)

As many as 70 percent of persons dying in the United States do not leave a will. Legally, dying without a will is called *intestacy* or dying *intestate.* And while a surprising number of men die without a will, the percentage is even greater among women. Intestacy has sometimes been described by astute businesspeople as the exact opposite of estate planning, and as we will see from the material that follows, almost all these people could have passed on more money or property to their heirs by using a will.

President Abraham Lincoln was one of the most famous examples of an individual who died intestate. Even though he was an able, careful lawyer, Mr. Lincoln was apparently so in-

---

[2]United States v. Perkins, 163 U.S. 625; In re Ogg's Estate, 54 N. W. 2nd 262.

[3]In re Uihleine's Estate, 68 N. W. 2d 816, 269 Wisc. 170.

volved in affairs of state that he never paused to realize that death
could overtake anyone at any time. Consequently, Lincoln's business and personal affairs were in a confused state at the time of his
assassination.

But most individuals who own any appreciable amount of
property do dispose of it by will, because a will almost always has
advantages and because dying intestate almost always has disadvantages. If there is no will, the law of the state where you die
specifies which of your heirs will receive your property and in
what proportions. The state laws on descent and distribution,
sometimes called the laws of *devise* and *descent,* rarely coincide
with the suppositions of the individual who dies without a will.
These laws of descent and distribution also vary considerably
from state to state.

A recent survey showed that more than 75 percent of adults
in several states could not *correctly* identify the specific relatives to
whom their property would pass if they died without a will. In
most instances, a husband intends to give some financial security
to his widow in the event he dies. The majority of people are
apparently under the impression that the surviving wife or husband will automatically receive all or most of the property that is
left. However, in a number of states, this is simply not true.
Under the laws in many jurisdictions, the wife is entitled to from
one-third to one-half of the husband's property. In some other
states, the wife's share is the same as that of each minor child;
thus if there are seven children, the wife would receive only
one-eighth of the estate. Of course, the wife could probably
qualify as guardian of the minor children and thereby have power
to distribute their funds. But in most states she would need a
court order to spend the children's money for anything but the
barest of necessities, and she would be closely supervised and
required to account for expenditures in detail. This involvment in
court matters often represents a loss of time by the surviving
widow; and the resulting court costs may eat heavily into estate
funds intended for the family.

Under the laws in other areas, the surviving wife would be required to share her husband's estate with the deceased husband's parents, brothers and sisters, or other relatives, if the couple had no children of their own. In some instances, a real injustice can result when one of the spouses dies without a will. In one actual case, a husband put all the couple's property in the wife's name, assuming that she would outlive him, but the wife died at an early age, leaving no will and no surviving children. Under the controlling state laws of devise and descent, half of the wife's estate went to her nearest blood relative, her mother (the husband's mother-in-law), and the remaining half of the wife's estate went to the deceased woman's husband. The end result was that the surviving husband got only half of the property that the couple had rightfully owned, while the husband's mother-in-law got the remaining half. In all likelihood, this was hardly what the couple had intended.

If a couple has minor children, there may be an even greater need for a will, because like anyone else, minors own the property that they inherit. But they are legally restricted in the use of that property until they come of legal age. If they inherit from an intestate parent, a legal guardian must be appointed, with accompanying costs for bonding of the guardian, and court supervision and accounting. Using available inherited money to send a deserving child to college may require a court order to cover the expenditure, but there is always a possibility that the supervising judge may turn down what appears to be a reasonable request to spend money on the child. An outright bequest from a deceased father to the mother, or a trust for the benefit of a child would avoid this guardianship difficulty, which may result from intestacy. It is therefore apparent that you should not die without a will, if you want to determine who receives your money or if you want to exercise control over how your bequests are used.

First it should be pointed out that it may take longer to handle the distribution of property when no will has been left. With, of course, some exceptions, the heirs are usually slower in receiving their inheritance when there is no will, and this delay often comes at a time when the heirs are in real need.

Secondly, someone must be appointed by the probate court to settle the estate of a person who dies intestate. The individual handling this responsibility (the *administrator*) is legally required to put up a bond. In most states this bond is one and one-half times the value of the estate—or more in some states. This bond is to insure that the administrator will not take some of the assets of the estate. The cost for a bond of this kind must be paid for out of the funds of the estate, thus using some of the money that may be needed by the deceased's wife and children. Under terms that may be set out in a will, this bond can be waived for this administrative person, called an *executor* or *executrix*. If the executor or executrix is a reliable relative or close friend, this bonding cost may be completely unnecessary.

For example, in 1979 the yearly premium on a probate bond of $150,000, to cover one and one-half times the value of an estate of $100,000, was $660 per year. An in the same year, the annual premium on a probate bond of $15 million, to cover one and one-half times the value of an estate of $10 million was $17,260 per year. This bonding requirement is sometimes a ridiculous safeguard, since the only heirs are often the surviving spouse and the deceased's children. In most instances, it is highly unlikely that a widow or widower who has been appointed administrator or administratrix of a spouse's estate would be required to post bond to insure that the children will not be cheated out of their inheritance.

There are a number of other costs and fees that may be assessed if the estate settlement is made by an administrator appointed by a court, rather than by an executor under the terms of a will. (Appointment of an administrator is discussed later in the text.) In a modest estate left without a will, estate shrinkage between death and final distribution of the property may amount to one-half.

If real property (real estate) is left and there is no will, the sale of this kind of property is under the detailed regulation of the probate court, and if a good offer for the purchase of estate property is received, it may expire before court approval is obtained. As previously indicated, court approval must be obtained to dispose of any property of a minor, unless provided otherwise by a will. This requirement for detailed court supervision may be waived by will, and the executor or executrix is authorized to dispose of it to the best advantage of the heirs. Under such a provision in a will, the executor is independent of court supervision. This is a so-called *nonintervention,* or *independent will*. If an executor or executrix is authorized by will to settle the estate without putting up bond, he or she is still personally liable for mishandling any of the assets of the estate.

Minor Children

If you leave minor children, and no guardian is named in a will, the judge will appoint someone as guardian, sometimes an individual that you would regard as completely unsuitable. In some instances, because the guardian may be a complete stranger, naming a guardian in your will becomes important, on the chance that both husband and wife are killed in an accident.

SUMMARY

Properly written, a will or trust agreement should leave the property to those the owner knows may need it and should have it. In addition, wills, trusts, and some other legal tools may be used to avoid unnecessary estate taxes and other unwanted costs. It may be surprising to some, but a good number of people say that the writing of a will gives peace of mind.

All this adds up to the fact that we should prepare a will, except in unusual circumstances.

2

What a Will Is, And What It Accomplishes

A *will* is the legal declaration or expression of an individual's wishes for the disposition of his or her property, to take effect after death. In the usual meaning of the word, it is a written document or instrument executed with the required formalities of law. It is sometimes called a *last will and testament* or simply a *testament.* When only personal property (such as clothing, car, jewelry, furniture, and the like) is disposed of, the instrument is sometimes called a *devise.* For our purposes, a will, devise, testament, or last will and testament are all the same thing.

As we have already noted, a will has technical differences that vary from state to state. Most basic requirements are uniform, but because of the differences that do exist, it is usually advisable to hire a local lawyer to draft one.

Courts and lawyers say that "a will speaks at the time of death." That means a will has no legal effect whatever during the maker's lifetime. Subject to change or complete withdrawal (legally called *revocation*) at any time, the courts look on a will as though executed immediately prior to the maker's death, but no legal rights are established (vested) until death has occurred.

WHY FORMAL REQUIREMENTS FOR WILLS WERE ESTABLISHED

The early English courts discovered that wills could be subject to all kinds of fraud, forgery, substitution, and manipulation. Would-be heirs came into the courts with increasing frequency and perjured themselves in oral testimony, declaring that the maker of a will had not intended to leave property to the individuals named in a written will. Beginning in the time of King Henry VIII, in 1540, the English Parliament passed laws regulating the ways in which wills could be prepared. Parliament continued to pass laws in this regard until 1837, and these regulations were gradually incorporated in various forms into law in the United States.[1]

In all states in this country, wills have specific, formal requirements that must be complied with exactly. Individuals frequently question why these legal formalities must be met, but following such procedures seems to have been the only way the courts could devise to minimize fraud and forgery. Too often courts are concerned with legal questions and not with solving people's problems. Even though there may not be a suggestion of fraud in the preparation or execution of a will, if formal require-

[1]This series of British laws has been known as the "Wills Act," or "The Statute of Wills," with one called "Lord Langdale's Act," Stat. 32 Henry VIII, c. 1 (1540) to 7 Wm. IV and 1 Vict. c. 26 (1837).

ments are not met, the document will not be accepted. The courts do not feel justified in overlooking specific statutory requirements, even to bring about substantial justice.

Any material alterations from the way the document was originally executed may cause a court to rule a will invalid. Alterations or changes in the will are not objectionable in themselves, if they occur at the time the will is made. It is almost always preferable to have the will retyped, rather than to make changes, because then the court is certain that the will reflects what the maker intended. The courts feel it is an unfair burden on them to try to determine who made changes, especially with the maker dead and witnesses hard to locate or also deceased. Incorporation into the will of a specific list of items, such as antique jewelry, art objects, or antiques, runs the risk of making an entire will invalid if the maker pulls out the will, adding or deleting items from the list after the time of execution.

NO SPECIFIC REQUIREMENTS TO THE WORDING OF A WILL

The exact wording or form of a will makes little difference. Any words may be used, as long as they show the intent of the maker to dispose of property, provided the formalities required by statute are met. The courts say that "a will is not a sheet of paper, nor a number of sheets or pages, but consists of the words written thereon."[2]

Wills have always shown the diversity of individual preferences. One of the shortest wills on file may be that written by an Englishman a generation or two ago. It reads: "I leave all my property to my wife, and no foolishness about it." Former President Calvin Coolidge's will was twenty-five words long, and one

[2]In re Golden's will, 300 N. Y. S. 737; in re Fowle's Estate. 290 N. W. 883, 292 Mich. 500.

of the longest wills on record was that of Mrs. Fred Cook of London, written in 1925. In disposing of an estate of $100,000, Mrs. Cook wrote a document of more than a thousand pages. Reportedly, the longest will ever offered for probate in the United States contained 95,940 words. A will may even be written in poetry, provided it satisfies the legal requirement that the maker's intent be clear.

A CONVENTIONAL WILL MUST BE IN WRITING

English and American courts have long required conventional, or so-called formal, wills to be in writing. Court holdings, however, have almost uniformly been to the effect that no will would be thrown out because of the quality of the writing or because of the type of writing materials used.

An early day English decision, which set the pattern that has been followed in American courts, is of a shipwrecked English sailor on a raft who scribbled his will on a piece of floating 2 × 4 planking from the breakup of his vessel. The maker of the will died of exposure a short time later, but a second sailor survived the shipwreck and carried the scribbled board back to England, where the water soaked board was accepted by the British probate court as a written will.

In a Canadian case in more recent times, a farmer was trapped in an isolated field when his tractor overturned. Seriously injured and knowing that he was likely to die before help could arrive, the farmer wrote a will. Apparently in great pain and without writing materials, he scratched out a short will on the underside of the tractor's fender before he died, which read: "In case I die in this mess I leave it all to the wife. Cecil George Harris."

One eccentric in Boston was informed that a valid will could be written on paper, parchment, cloth, or wood. In preparing his will shortly thereafter, this individual wrote out his bequests on a door in the bedroom of his home, and, when he died, the door was taken from its hinges and carried into court for probate.

Neither legislatures nor courts in the United States have ever specified just what kind of writing must be used in preparing a will. In the cases that have been appealed, the courts have accepted wills that were written in lead pencil, written partly in pencil and party in ink, and even begun in ink and completed by typewriter as long as they were properly signed and witnessed. Acceptable wills have also included documents written on two sides of paper.[3]

The general principle of law is that a document will be admitted to probate as a conventional will when it was prepared in any kind of legible writing, hand printing, or typing, and when it was apparent that the maker's intent was to prepare that particular writing as a will.[4]

All these comments pertain to a *conventional* will. As we will see in subsequent material, a special type of will called a *holographic will* has specific requirements concerning the manner in which it must be written.

The English and American courts have also said that the writing of a will need not necessarily be undertaken in the English language.[5] So long as the foreign language is clear in meaning and conforms to other statutory requirements, the will is valid. To hold otherwise would be for the courts to rule that an individual cannot make an acceptable will because that person is not able to read and write English fluently.

In the preparation of your own will, the safest way is to have it written on numbered sheets of paper that are uniform in size. Some courts in the past have raised serious questions about ac-

[3]Stuck v. Howard, 104 So. 500, 312 Ala. 184.
[4]Hays v. Marschall, 48 S. W. 2d 540, 243 Ky. 392.
[5]Heupel v. Heupel, 174 P. 2d 850, 197 Okla. 567. For an acceptable will written in Italian, see in re Estate of Cuneo, 60 Cal. 2d 196, 384 P. 2d 1.

cepting wills written on two sizes or grades of paper. Similarly, doubt may be raised as to authenticity if one page is written on pica type and the next page is prepared on elite type. You should avoid raising doubts in the judge's mind as to whether pages have been substituted for original writing. To make it clear that nothing has been left out or substituted, a statement can be included in the will similar to the following:

> This will consists of this page and _____ pages, written on one side of each sheet. I have affixed my signature to the bottom line of each sheet.

Then the pages should be numbered.

Some legal uncertainty may also arise when a will refers to an outside document in connection with bequests or provisions. As the minimum requirement, the courts insist on positive identification of the outside document. For example, the maker of a will gives property to twenty individuals named in a letter dated April 15, 1979, signed by the testator and placed in the testator's locked safe deposit box #1037 at State Mutual Savings and Loan Office, Belmont Shore Branch, Long Beach, California. The names, addresses, telephone numbers and other vital information are then listed in the letter deposited in the safe deposit box. Lawyers call a technique of this kind *incorporation by reference.* In short, the outside letter is incorporated into the will. Some attorneys feel that the safest approach is to have the outside document or outside material actually typed into the text of the will itself, rather than to leave any room for doubt.

Paper, of course, is the medium on which a will is normally recorded. An American woman wrote a will on wallpaper in 1902—a will that was duly held to be valid. Another woman wrote her will on two paper napkins, and the will prepared by John M. Locke, M.D., was written on a medical prescription pad. In 1960, a hospital patient suffering a terminal illness disposed of his $6-million estate by a statement written on the back of his

nursing chart at the hospital. A will filed for probate in Los
Angeles Superior Court in 1950 had been prepared by Mrs. Beth
A. Baer, a blind woman, Although Mrs. Baer was able to write
but could not see, she wrote until her pen ran out of ink. Not
realizing that the ink had ceased to flow, she pressed on with her
pen. Subsequently, Clark Sellers, a handwriting expert, was able
to make out words from the indentations on the paper made from
the pressure of the empty pen. The will was accepted by the
court.

WHO HAS A RIGHT
TO MAKE A WILL?

All states require an individual to have attained a specified
age in order to write a valid will. This limitation varies from the
age of 14 in some states to 21 in others, but most states require
the maker to be either 18 or 21. Some states permit an individual
of 18 to write a will disposing of personal property, but require
the maker to be 21 if the property includes any real estate.

Because of these variations regarding the minimum age at
which an individual can make a will, it is suggested that you
inquire locally through a lawyer if there is any doubt about age
requirements. No state has a limitation prohibiting a person of
advanced age from writing a will, but if an individual is senile
and mental requirements cannot be satisfied, the will may not be
accepted for probate by the courts.

In most states a person sentenced to life imprisonment is
said to be "civilly dead." Such a conviction carries with it loss of
the right to vote and other privileges, although some state courts
also hold that a will written by one who is civilly dead is invalid.

But the right to make a will is not limited to any social class
or monetary distinction. Quite universally, the U.S. courts ac-

cept a will from any adult of sound mind. As said by one judge, the individual making a will "does not have to be a literarian, a financial genius, an athlete, or an expert cook."[6]

In words of another court, the maker can be "illiterate, disagreeable, untidy, unsocial, miserly, and with unjust prejudices and religious fanaticism."[7] To carry it somewhat further, the courts are in general agreement that a will must still be recognized even though it exhibits "lack of a keen mind, or distress in memory" or "somewhat less mental capacity than that required to carry on business . . ."

The general test demanded of the courts is that the maker appreciate and understand the nature and consequences of his or her act in giving away property as a gift.

WHEN LEGALLY POSSIBLE, THE COURTS UPHOLD A WILL

Insofar as legally permissible, the courts strive to uphold the validity of a will. This is especially so if the document contains the essential characteristics of a will. Judges frequently point out that they are reluctant to undo after death what the property owner sought to accomplish. But the courts also note that one must be careful to satisfy formal requirements.[8]

Usually a provision in a will is struck down by the courts only after the judges have made every effort to find a reasonable construction or meaning that can be placed on the maker's words.

[6]In re Wiltzius' Estate, 253 P. 2 954, 42 Wash. 2d 149.
[7]Walsh v. Fairhead, 219 S. W. 2d 941, 215 Ark. 218.
[8]In re Donnelly's Estate, 188 So. 108, 137 Fla. 459; in re Hamilton's Estate, 174 P. 2d 301, 26 Wash. 2d 363.

COURTS SUPPORT WHAT THE MAKER (TESTATOR) INTENDED

Once the will has been upheld as valid by being admitted to probate, the courts interpret the provisions in the will to give effect, as nearly as possible, to the maker's probable intent at the time the will was executed. The problem here is that the requests in the will may be subject to more than one interpretation, and the court may be forced to turn to outside sources in ascertaining this meaning.

A will may contain eccentric or bizarre bequests and still be upheld, so long as the bequests can be reasonably fulfilled and are not illegal. The will of a wealthy old Scotsman provided that each of his two daughters was to receive her weight in one-pound British bank notes. The will was upheld without question, the oldest daughter receiving £51,200, while the younger received £57,344. On the other hand, an American court struck down as impractical the bequest of an eccentric who left $100,000 to a scientist of his acquaintance for experiments in turning the ocean into orangeade.

Of course, the courts will not uphold a provision in a will that would require illegal activity, or dealing in contraband. In a similar manner, some other bequests would not be allowed as a matter of public policy. Examples of actual provisions in wills that have been struck down include bequests like the following:

1. "One thousand dollars to break Mace King out of Brushy Mountain state pen."

2. ". . . to set up a first class gambling casino."

3. Or a bequest by a deceased husband giving his wife to his best friend, "since she is the best damn lay in the country."

Many courts uphold a bequest of money that will be paid from the deceased's estate if a relative does not marry a named individual who was disliked by the deceased. It is a somewhat different matter, however, to leave a bequest to a relative "on condition that she immediately divorce her husband." The courts generally hold that such a bequest is unacceptable, as it is against public policy to sanction legal action that could break up a home.

WHO SHOULD SIGN A WILL?

Every adult with any property should make a will as soon as possible. Since this may be the most important legal document that many of us ever sign, it should not be delayed, even though many individuals put off the execution. After the details needed for drafting have been given to a lawyer, with the will not yet being signed, clients frequently delay return to the lawyer's office. Often there is a personal resistance to the planning and execution of a will, because the act of signing smacks of preparation for death, and most of us are not yet ready for this. Some of this reluctance may be a natural unwillingness to get involved in anything that seems to be court related.

A husband may find that little is accomplished by discussions at home, since his wife does not like to think about the possibility of his sudden departure. And it may be painful to insist on discussions concerning an expensive home operation that might be discontinued if the husband's income suddenly came to an end.

Other individuals are simply intimidated by the whole procedure, stating that they are in good health. But since accidents and unforeseen illness may happen at any time, even young adults need wills. Other individuals put off making a will, stating that most of their property is jointly owned. They reason that this property will automatically pass to their surviving partner without going through a will settlement in a probate court. This reasoning is valid in some instances, but, in other family situations, this solution may not consider the resulting tax problems.

Another common misconception is that the responsibility

for making a will is the husband's exclusive problem, and in many instances it is just as important for the wife to also have a valid will. This is especially true when wives may have as much property as the husband and when they may have accumulated an estate from earnings, inheritance, or investments. In so-called community property states, the wife's financial worth is commonly as great as that of the husband.

The cost of an attorney's fee is also sometimes given as a reason for not writing a will. While the lawyer's fee increases with the complexity of the document and the specific problems involved, a lawyer usually gives an accurate estimate of cost over the telephone. He may write an uncomplicated will for a reasonably flat fee that is justified in view of the benefits to be expected from the will.

3
Writing a Conventional, Or Formal, Will

In one sense, all we can say for a will is that it is a writing expressing your desires about how you want your property disposed of. It is up to you and your lawyer to give it validity—that is, to make it legally effective.

As we have noted, there are minor technical differences from state to state in the preparation of a conventional or formal will. The laws of every state insist on such formalities, to make certain that the will is actually that of the person whose property is being disposed of. After all, there is no way we can call the deceased back to make sure. So the courts and legislatures evolved these formalities to insure a strong likelihood of authenticity. It should be kept in mind, then, that while these legal rules are burdensome, they were designed for the benefit of the writer of the will.

BASIC REQUIREMENTS

There are four basic formalities that must be complied with in all states:

1. The maker of the will, the testator, must have had the intent to actually dispose of property by will. This is the requirement of the courts that the lawyers call *testamentary intent*.

2. The maker of the will must have met the individual state requirements about being of the required age and of sound mind at the time the will was made. This is what the lawyers and the courts call *legal capacity*.

3. The maker must not have signed under duress, fraud, mistake, or undue influence. If the testator put his or her signature to the will under the impression that the matter was a practical joke, or at the point of a gun, then the document is not a valid will. Likewise, if the maker signed without reading and in the mistaken notion that the instrument was a business contract, then it would be rejected on the legal grounds of *mistake*. Similarly, if a will was signed under undue influence, when the maker was not really able to exercise clear judgment, the instrument would be invalid. This problem will be considered subsequently in more detail.

4. The maker must have signed the will in the presence and within the view of the required number of witnesses, who also signed in accordance with statutory requirements in that state.

Testamentary Intent

The legal reasoning behind this refusal to accept a fake or sham will to probate is that the maker simply did not have the required testamentary intent. For example, a will that was intended as a prop in a stage play would not be admitted to probate if the facts surrounding its preparation were made known to the probate court. This rejection would be made by the court, in spite of the recitation in the document itself that it was the "valid last will and testament" of a stated person. A will signed at the point of a gun would not satisfy the legal requirement of intent. The maker would simply have lacked necessary intent to make a valid will. In a somewhat similar situation, a probate court would decline to admit a will that had been executed solely for the purpose of inducing the named beneficiary of the will (legatee) to indulge in sexual relations with the maker.[1]

As a side issue, note that the courts will not usually allow oral testimony to take precedence over statements made on the face of a written instrument. But most courts will allow oral evidence to explain away the circumstances under which a will was executed. In a few states, however, there have been court holdings to the effect that statements in the body of a will are conclusive if the will was properly prepared (signed before witnesses, and so on). These legal holdings result from the court's well-grounded fear that some persons might testify falsely in order to profit from the maker's estate.

No Testamentary Intent If Property Is to Be Given in the Future. The courts generally agree that the necessary testamentary intent is not present unless it is a desire to transfer a gift immediately. In a typical case involving this point, a wealthy man wrote a letter, stating: "I'm going to make a will, leaving all my property to you." When this writing was not allowed as a will, the recipient of the letter appealed to a higher court in Kentucky. The court ruled that these words were a mere statement of intent for future action, and not a declaration of testamentary intent.[2]

But an instrument may be construed as a valid will if it contains a requirement that a specific condition must exist prior

[1]Clarke v. Ransom, 50 Cal. 595.
[2]Nelson v. Nelson, 235 Ky. 189; Appeal of Scott, 147 Pa. 89.

to the document being given effect as a will. For example, the courts hold that there is testamentary intent on the part of the writer of a statement such as the following: "This will shall be effective only in the event my wife predeceases me."

Legal (Mental) Capacity and the Required Legal Age

To have legal capacity, the maker of a will must have attained the age required by state law and must have been of sound mind at the time the will was executed. It is the mental condition that controls, so long as the physical state does not seriously affect the mind.

In one old will the maker wrote:

This is my last will and testament which I make, being sound in mind but utterly ruined in health.

The courts in a few states place the burden of proving mental competency on the party who offers the will for probate. But by far the majority of state courts say that every will submitted for probate carries with it a rebuttable presumption of mental competency, which, of course, has the effect of placing the burden of proving mental incompetency on the individual contesting the will.

From court decisions in these cases, it is obvious that testamentary capacity may be a variable thing, depending on all the surrounding circumstances. Most courts set up four tests for determining mental capability:

1. The maker of the will (testator) must have the ability (legal capacity) to understand the relationship between himself or herself and that individual's natural heirs. This means between the testator and "those who ought to be the natural objects of his or her bounty," as said by the courts.

2. The maker must understand the nature and extent of his or

her property. This is a general understanding of the estate. A rancher, for example, would not need to know how many cows he actually owns, and an investor does not need to know whether he or she is the owner of 11 or 13 shares of U.S. Steel stock.

3. The maker must have actual knowledge that he or she is executing a will.

4. The maker must have the capacity to evaluate the facts sufficiently to form some kind of orderly plan for the distribution of the property.

Signing the Will

In many countries of the world, the signing of a will is a ritual—a ceremony. After all, it confers a bit of immortality by allowing the maker to control property beyond life itself. The moods exhibited by makers frequently vary from the apprehensive to the amusing.

United States courts uniformly insist that a will must be signed by the maker in order to be accepted as valid. But the courts allow a great deal of latitude here. An individual who never learned to write can merely sign with an "X" if witnesses are present to verify the signing. This same procedure will be permitted by the courts for a maker who is blind and unable to write.

In some instances the individual making the will may be so old that he or she cannot actually write a firm, legible signature. In cases of this kind, the courts have usually said it is satisfactory for someone else to sign at the direction of the maker. In addition, wills have usually been approved in instances where the maker signed in his or her adopted name, or signed by an alias or assumed name that had been commonly used throughout the community. In other instances, the will has been approved when signed only as "Father," "Aunt Mary," with initials, or with an abbreviation such as "Chas. King."[3]

One court held that the requirement for signing had been met by an individual who affixed his signature by rubber stamp. But other courts have held that this was getting too far away from the legislative requirement that every will must be signed. In one case a printed monogram of the maker, attached to the will, was held insufficient as a signature, "since it was not in the maker's handwriting."[4]

To keep the possibility of legal controversy to an absolute minimum, the person making a will should recite his or her full and complete name, which is called his or her *legal* name. If another name is used anywhere in the will, the maker should precede that other name with his or her correct name and a statement such as: "also known in the community as _____."

Where the Signature Must Appear on the Will. The laws in a number of states specify that the maker's signature must be placed at the end of the instrument before the will can be held valid. Trying to uphold validity where possible, courts in a number of other states allow the signature to appear in the introduction, in the caption, or even in the body of the will.[5]

Dating the Will. There is a legal requirement in all states that the will must be dated, but some courts have held that this merely means a date must be established to the satisfaction of the court. If the signing at a particular time can be established by other means, this will be sufficient. For example, testimony from the lawyer who prepared the will, testifying from his office notes and files as to the day the work was performed and the will

[3]In re Kimmel's Estate, 123 A. 405, 278 Pa. 435; Estate of Button, 209 Cal. 325; 31 A.L.R. 678.
[4]Pounds v. Litaker, 235 N. C. 746.
[5]Estate of Morgan, 200 Cal. 400.

signed, would be adequate for acceptance.[6] But to be safe, your will should be dated at the time it is made.

Witnesses to the Will

Beginning with the Statute of Frauds in 1541, early English laws required wills to be signed by witnesses as well as by the maker, thus the intent here was to eliminate dishonesty. When American colonists brought law to this country, the same requirements for witnesses were continued. All states in the United States today have statutory requirements that at least two witnesses must sign, with some states requiring three.

The purpose in requiring witnesses to sign the will is to have someone available for the probate court in case it was ever necessary to prove that the will was signed by the maker. The witness would also be able to give an evaluation concerning whether the maker was being coerced or was of sound mind at the time the will was executed.

Obviously, then, it is preferable to select as a witness someone who is likely to be alive after your death, and it is also desirable to have someone who can be easily located, if that should be necessary. Individuals who move about a great deal or who are subject to regular transfers may be hard to locate after a few years have passed. A noted Hollywood star had his will witnessed by two musicians in a travelling jazz band. When the will was offered for probate, one witness could not be located. The second was located living in an American colony deep in the interior of Mexico. Persuading the witness to come testify before the probate court was a problem. Proving the validity of the Hollywood star's signature was expensive and the settlement of the estate was delayed. The moral of this, of course, is that you should make it easy on your executor by providing witnesses who are likely to outlive you and who will be easy to locate.

[6]In re Gray's Estate, 201 P. 2d 392, 89 Cal. App. 478.

Almost all states have statutes providing that relatives may not serve as witnesses and that the witnesses utilized must be individuals other than persons who may benefit under the terms of the will.

A case that received considerable newspaper publicity in California was the so-called "pettycoat will." In that case, a wealthy man in a Los Angeles hospital allegedly asked the nurses on duty for paper to write a will. Unable to find paper, one of the nurses allowed the testator to scribble a brief will on the white pettycoat she was wearing. In this will the testator left the bulk of his estate to a relative, and he also added a bequest of ten thousand dollars to each of the two nurses. Unable to find other witnesses, the nurses had both signed in that capacity. A short time later the testator died, and in a will contest that resulted, the jury held the will to be genuine. But the judge threw the will out, since under California law, beneficiaries cannot sign as witnesses. The language used in some state laws is that a witness to the will "cannot be beneficially interested." It is generally held by the courts that what this means is that a witness cannot be one who is to receive a direct pecuniary or monetary interest.[7]

Another requirement of law is that the witnesses must all know that the document in question is the maker's will. Most state laws say, however, that the witnesses do not necessarily need to be informed of the terms of the will. There is a difference in opinion in other states that require all witnesses to be told of the terms of the will.[8]

Statutes in some localities require all witnesses to sign in the presence of the testator, and a number of states specify that this signing by the witnesses must be in the immediate presence of each other, as well as in the immediate presence of the testator. To remove any possibility of doubt at a later time, the maker and required witnesses should all sign within the immediate view and

[7]California Probate Code, Section 109, is typical of the law in a number of states.

[8]In re Heavener's Estate, 246 P. 720, 118 Ore. 308.

presence of each other, with no appreciable time lag between signatures.

CLARITY IN THE WILL— SAYING WHAT YOU MEAN

Costly lawsuits and serious family quarrels sometimes result from a poorly drafted will containing obscure language. For example, a father's will directed the executor to "give $10,000 to my two daughters, Ann and Marie." It was only natural that the executor had doubts as to whether each daughter was to receive $10,000, or whether this sum was to be split between them. A judge summed it up when he said, "When life ends you are of no assistance in explaining what was meant in your will. It has got to speak for itself—on its face."

When ambiguity is found, courts try to solve this problem through established principles of will construction:

> The paramount (legal) rule in the construction of wills, to which all other rules must yield, is that a will is to be construed according to the intention of the testator as expressed therein, and this intention must be given effect as far as possible.[9]

The courts also say:

> . . . When an uncertainty arises upon the face of a will as to the meaning of any of its provisions, the testator's intent is to be ascertained from the words of the will, but the circumstances of the execution thereof may be taken into consideration, *excluding* the oral declarations of the testator as to his intentions.[10]

[9]Estate of Wilson, 184 Cal. 63, 193 P. 581.
[10]Estate of Salmonski, 38 Cal. 2d 199, 238 P. 2d 966.

If the language of the will is unequivocal and definite on its face, the courts will not permit outside testimony about what the testator intended. If outside verbal testimony is allowed to prevail in this type of situation, every will made will be subject to serious dispute. This would frequently lead to a false interpretation of a legal instrument.[11]

In one will, the testator left a valuable piece of property to the "Boy Guides of America," actually intending to leave the property to the Boy Scouts of America as a summer camp ground. There actually was an organization called Boy Guides of America, and the court awarded the property to this group, rather than to the Boy Scouts of America. The court said that to do otherwise would do violence to the exact, specific bequest of the maker. The court indicated, however, that if there had been no organization called "Boy Guides of America," the bequest would have been indefinite and not understandable without the benefit of verbal testimony, which is called *parol* evidence by lawyers, to explain what was really meant.[12]

Fine legal distinctions may be involved here. In another case a testator devised lot #10, Tract 403, to a relative. It turned out that there was a lot #10, but the testator did not own lot #10. He actually owned another lot. The court ruled that the testator did not actually own the property he attempted to give away, and that the bequest was void. Outside evidence would not be permitted to show that the testator owned a lot with a similar number. But if it was found that there was no lot #10, Tract 403, the courts would say that the will was still ambiguous. Then, verbal testimony (parol evidence) would be admitted to show just what the testator actually meant. If, in either instance, the testator had prefaced his description of the property by saying, "I devise lot #10, Tract 403, located in Lamb's Canyon,

[11]Universal Sales Corp. v. California, 20, Cal. 2d 751, 128 P. 2d 665.
[12]Symonds v. Sherman, 219 Cal. 249.

Utah, . . ." the court would say the ambiguity could be resolved by verbal testimony to show what the testator really intended.[13]

In summarizing this problem, one court explained the law as follows:

> Broadly speaking, there are two classes of wills presenting . . . ambiguities [where] . . . resort to extrensic evidence [outside verbal testimony] is permissible. The one class is where there are two or more persons or things exactly measuring up to the description and conditions of the will . . . The other class is where no person or thing exactly answers the declarations and descriptions of the will, but where two or more persons or things in part though imperfectly do so answer.[14]

The moral of all this seems to be that the maker of a will should reexamine it objectively, making certain that a complete stranger could clearly understand it. In addition, the will should say just what you mean.

A lawyer is human too and can make errors, but a lawyer is far less likely to use imprecise language than someone who writes his or her own will. The maker should closely check the exact wording of the lawyer's typed version.

[13]Patch v. White, 117 U. S. 201; Aliver v. Henderson, 121 Ga. 836.
[14]Estate of Donnellan, 164 Cal. 14, 127 P. 166.

4

Disinheritance: Bequests to Other Than Ordinary Heirs

DISINHERITING NATURAL HEIRS

For hundreds of years, individuals have expressed doubt that the courts would uphold a maker's will. Demosthenes, the famous Greek statesman and orator (384 B.C.–322 B.C.), pointed out that it was customary in the last paragraph of early-day Greek wills to call down all sorts of vile curses on anyone who attempted to alter bequests in the body of the will. The inscription on a tombstone in an old English churchyard contains the commentary: "Man heapeth up riches, but he knoweth not who shall gather them."

Legally, the courts say that within limits the right to pass on property carries with it the right to disinherit. Benjamin Franklin cut off his son William from a bequest of some land holdings of negligible value in Nova Scotia. Franklin explained in his will that in part William had

> . . . acted against me in the last Revolutionary War, which is of public notoriety, will account for my leaving him no more of an estate that he endeavored to deprive me of.

But the courts in most states will not allow an individual to inherit from the estate of a husband or wife who was murdered by the other party to the marriage.[1] This principle has not been upheld in all courts, however.

This exclusion was based on the old idea of the English law that no one should be allowed to benefit by doing wrong. In the event of murder, most states now have laws giving the estate to the lawful heirs, excluding the murderer.[2]

FORCED HEIRSHIP LAWS

A number of states have so-called *forced heirship* statutes, requiring that a certain percentage of any individual's estate must be passed on to specific heirs, such as a wife or children. The forced heirship share may amount to one-third, to one-half, or to some other specific percentage of the estate. These statutory rights are usually limited by the courts to such property as was owned by the decedent at the time of death. In other words,

---

[1]Riggs v. Palmer, 22 N. E. 188, 115 N. Y. 506; Succession of Trahant, 76 So. 2d 919, 226 La. 653.

[2]Floyd v. Franklin, 251 Ala. 15, involved a wife who was convicted of manslaughter, but was nevertheless permitted to inherit from the husband she killed.

conveyance, which is a property transfer by deed, prior to death is ordinarily effective in cutting off the rights of the surviving spouse or other heirs. If the testator does not have any heirs that fall into this class, then there is no such requirement. Forced heirship statutes apply, even though the heirs in question may be specifically disinherited in a will. In states with such statutes, a surviving wife or husband has the right to take either the amount specified in the will or that provided by the heirship statutes, whichever is greater.

These forced heirship statutes originated from early English law, at a time when married women had no right to own property. This inability to own property often worked an extreme hardship on a widow, who might be left with nothing. To correct this situation to some extent, the English law worked out the property right of a widow that became known as *dower.* This consisted of a one-third interest for the widow's life in all the real property (real estate) owned by the husband during his lifetime. The wife had this right, unless she had signed it away, even if the husband had already sold the property before his death. This legal right was called *dower,* and upon her husband's death, the widow became known as a *dowager.*

This right to dower still exists in a number of states in the United States, but the right does not come into being until the death of the husband. If the wife did not sign away her dower right when the husband sold property, the wife may come back against the purchaser to enforce the right, even though many years may have elapsed.

Eventually, women in England were given the right to own property individually. The widower's right to a life estate in the deceased wife's property came to be called *curtesy.* (A *life estate* is an interest in property that lasts only for the duration of the life of some specified individual. When dower is involved, property right would last during the wife's lifetime. See *life estate* in the glossary.) Both of these rights of dower and curtesy still exist in various forms in some states in this country, but in some other states, these old rights have been replaced by forced heirship statutes.

LIMITS ON CHARITABLE BEQUESTS

The courts usually say that a charitable bequest is one to individuals, organizations, or associations in a non-profit category. The aims and accomplishments of a charitable bequest must be for educational, political, religious, or general social interest to mankind.[3] The ultimate recipients may include the community as a whole, or some class from a part of it, unascertainable as to persons. It must be for the welfare of mankind or for those unable to help themselves, without profit to anyone. A donation to a specific individual would be a gift under the federal tax laws. To constitute a charity, there must be uncertainty regarding beneficiaries.

A number of states have laws that limit the percentage of the estate that may be willed to charity if there are specific heirs living. Laws of this kind have a background that goes far back in English history to the latter part of the Middle Ages. At this time, church officials commonly put pressure for bequests on wealthy individuals who were facing death. Under circumstances of this kind, many testators were inclined to give everything to the church, in hopes of increasing their chances in the "life beyond." Another issue here was that the medieval church had become the owner of about half of all the land in England, and, as a result, there was no land available for the small landowners. Fearing this great accumulation of wealth and power in the hands of politically oriented churchmen, English kings also realized

[3]City of Houston v. Scottish Rite Benevolent Assn., 230 S. W. 978; Goode's Administrator v. Goode, 38 S. W. 2d 691.

there would be no property to tax if these land acquisitions continued. Consequently, in 1279 A.D., the English kings began the passage of laws to limit the amount of property that could be willed to charity. Another reason for the acceptance of these laws was that testators frequently left their heirs in poverty because of a last-minute effort to save their souls.

Some states in the United States still have so-called *mortmain statutes,* based on the old English laws. These mortmain statutes usually restrict the percentage that can be left to charity to one-half or less of the value of the estate.[4] If there are no living heirs, it may all be left to charity. Laws in some other states prohibit any gift whatever to charity if the will was executed within a specified short period before death (such as 30 days). These are the so-called *fear of hell* statutes.[5]

UNUSUAL BEQUESTS IN A WILL

In the words of one judge, unless there are forced heirship statutes, property may be willed with

> . . . unfettered discretion. It may be given to those who are strangers, without regard to natural or moral claims, cutting off relatives and natural heirs in a way that could be considered unjust by the standards of people . . . And the testator may do this even out of revenge.

There are of course, limitations as to what you can bequest. An individual who owes money may not defeat creditors and leave them upaid, simply by willing away the money or property

---

[4]In re Randall's Estate, 194 P. 2d. 709, 86 Cal. App. 2 d. 422.
[5]Florida Statutes, Section 731.19.

that would be used to pay off debts. The deceased's debts must be paid first, insofar as the deceased left money or property to satisfy them. Courts say bequests in a will must be within reason. In one old case, because the deceased had a fear that "he might be disturbed in his eternal rest," he set up a trust fund to pay for an armed, uniformed guard to patrol his grave indefinitely. The probate court refused to allow the executor to make this expenditure, stating that it would be a needless dissipation of assets. It did, however, permit the payment of a reasonable fee for permanent care for the grave site.

Some lawyers frankly advise clients that the writing of a will is not the place for the exhibition of excessive eccentricity. Wills are not successfully contested in a great number of cases, but this is often because of the careful precautions taken by the lawyer who prepared the will. Yet if the testator insists on making highly unusual bequests or grants to unconventional people or causes, there is an increased likelihood that the will may be broken.

What sometimes happens in unusual cases is that the very nature of the bequest is so eccentric that the judge or jury may be easily convinced that the maker could not have been mentally sound. As a practical matter, some lawyers feel that unusual bequests should be explained to some extent in the text of the will, if this can be done logically. Standing unexplained, a bequest of several thousand dollars to establish a refuge for desert turtles could be argued as an indication that the maker of the will was mentally unsound at the time the will was made. But the bequest might be understood by a judge or jury if the testator noted in his will that he was a trained biologist who had spent a great deal of time in studying this species. It could also be explained in the will that this bequest culminated a lifetime of interest in this kind of wildlife.

Some attorneys take whatever steps they can in advance to build a case for upholding the will. In all states the test of testamentary capacity is whether, at the time of execution of the will, the maker comprehended the extent of his or her property and the persons naturally entitled to the maker's bounty. Accordingly, the lawyer who drafts the will keeps a comprehensive set of notes in file that describe the entire transaction. The lawyer may keep a written record of the exact questions asked the client making the will, along with specific answers. Today, some lawyers actually record the entire interview on a tape recorder, especially if the client is lucid and logical throughout. If it is obvious that the maker of the will has described the extent of property involved and gives specific reasons for unusual requests, then the chances for successfully contesting the will are greatly reduced. However, some judges frankly state that favor will be shown by the courts to the natural heirs and next of kin.

BEQUESTS TO PETS

Perhaps the most common types of unusual bequests are those made by pet lovers. Dogs and cats come in for the largest share of gifts, but other animals are sometimes remembered. In most instances of this kind, the bequest is left in trust to some individual who is to care for the pet so long as it lives. A case of this kind involved the estate of Thelma L. Russell, a California resident who died in 1965. In Mrs. Russell's will, which was accepted by the probate court, the following bequest was made:

March 18, 1957

. . . I leave everything I own Real & Personal to Chester H. Quinn & Roxy Russell.

Thelma L. Russell

The reverse side of the will reads:

My ($10.) Ten dollar gold piece & diamonds I leave to Georgia Nan Russell. Alverata, Georgia (sic).

Chester H. Quinn, a close personal friend of Thelma L.

Russell, stood in a relation of personal trust and confidence toward her. In a petition to serve as executor of the will, Chester H. Quinn advised the court that the beneficiaries under the will were he and Roxy Russell, a 9-year-old Airdale dog residing at 4422 Palm Avenue, La Mesa, California.

Georgia Nan Russell Hembree, niece and only living natural heir of Thelma L. Russell sued for that half of the estate left to the Airdale dog. Hembree's lawyer pointed out that Section 27 of the California Probate code enumerated those entitled to take by will, and stated that "dogs are not included among those listed. . . ." Attorneys for Quinn maintained that the testatrix had intended to leave the entire estate, except for the $10 gold piece and the diamonds, to Quinn who was to care for the dog. Quinn offered evidence to show that this was Thelma Russell's intent. This matter came up on appeal to the Supreme Court of California. In the decision, the court commented on the interpretation that should be given to words in a will:

> . . . a court cannot determine whether the terms of the will are clear and definite in the first place until it considers the circumstances under which the will was made so that the judge may be placed in the position of the testator whose language [the judge] is interpeting.

The court ruled however, that the only reasonable construction that could be given to Thelma Russell's words was that she intended to give her property to Quinn and the dog equally, which makes them tenants in common. Since a dog could not be a beneficiary under a will according to the California statute (Probate Code Section 27), that portion of the will pertaining to the dog was invalid. The dog's share was then awarded to Hembree.[6] The maker of another will filed in California left everything to a friend for the support and maintenance of the deceased's favorite riding horse.

[6]Estate of Russell, 69 Cal. 2d 200, 444 P 2d 353.

BEQUESTS TO THE
U.S. GOVERNMENT

The United States government also receives money from bequests of many individuals. These gifts frequently come from foreign-born citizens who have prospered in this country. Gifts to the government seem to increase during wartime, especially during a politically popular war.

The great Supreme Court Justice, Oliver Wendell Holmes, lived to be 85, but, when he died, Holmes had outlived his wife and all his relatives. Since the original investments in his sizable estate had come wholly from his government salary, Holmes willed back his property to the United States.

One unusual will was that of an Idaho businessman who left most of his property to his widow, appointing the widow to serve as executrix. Little attention was paid to an advertisement the widow placed in a Boise, Idaho newspaper. Those readers who saw the ad did not believe it, since the widow offered to sell a late model Cadillac with low mileage for only $50. Eventually, someone answered the advertisement and bought the car. It turned out that the husband had specified in his will that the car, or the proceeds from its sale, were to go to a girlfriend that the widow had never been aware of during her husband's lifetime.

CUTTING OFF THE HEIR WHO
CONTESTS YOUR WILL

Sometimes will makers insert a provision that cuts off anyone who contests the will or that leaves only a trifling sum to such an individual. If there is serious likelihood that an heir may contest the terms, the will should be drafted by an attorney in the state where the document is to be offered for probate. State laws differ, some having strict technical requirements for a provision of this kind and some requiring forfeit of the bequest by the

44

person contesting the will to a named individual or class of persons, such as "to my other sons and daughters." The courts sometimes call this a *gift over* to the other heirs. It may not be sufficient for an individual to merely state that "the bequest to anyone contesting this will is to be forfeited and included in the residuary portion of my estate." In some states, an heir may be cut off with a mere bequest of one dollar, but this should be done only on the advice of your lawyer.

LIBELING THE DISINHERITED HEIR

Lawyers are almost always in agreement in urging clients not to make a libelous statement in a will for any reason. Such a statement usually concerns an heir who is being disinherited. For example, a testator should not include a paragraph in a will like the following:

> I leave nothing to my brother, Warren Wiggledon, as it is well known that he left his wife and small children without support, beat his wife without cause, and is a confirmed drunk and dope addict.

If Warren Wiggledon wins a lawsuit against the estate for libel, the costs of the judgment must be paid by the estate. This, in effect, takes money from heirs that the testator had intended to favor over Warren Wiggledon.

INSANE DELUSIONS

The general rule of law is that a person may have some insane delusions or mental impairment and still have the required mental capacity to prepare an orderly plan of disposal. The courts have often pointed out, here, that 100 percent sanity may be a myth. If an individual's insane delusions are such that they interfere with that person's ability to formulate an orderly plan for disposal of property, then the insane delusions destroy legal capacity to write a valid will.

Almost all individuals have some unusual or unorthodox beliefs. Neither jealousy, nor prejudice, nor peculiar religious beliefs, standing alone, will be admitted as evidence of mental derangement sufficient to regard the maker of a will as mentally unbalanced. As stated in other words previously, the test usually applied by the courts is that even an insane delusion will not void a will, unless the property disposition scheme used in the will was based on one of these insane delusions. Even if an individual disposition or bequest is based on an insane delusion, most courts hold that this fact will not invalidate the remainder of the will. The particular grant or gift will be struck out, if the specific delusion runs to that particular beneficiary or gift.[7]

In defining an *insane delusion,* the courts say that it is a belief to which the testator adheres, against all reason, argument, or evidence. In other terms, it is a belief in facts that do not exist and that no rational individual believed existed. An individual's belief can be completely illogical and still not amount to an insane delusion. The controlling idea is whether there were any facts from which the maker of the will could have reached his or her conviction. If some fact existed that would have permitted the incorrect conclusion, regardless of whether it was reached improperly, the belief would not be an insane delusion.

Completely groundless beliefs—that nineteen relatives had been stealing from the testator when they all lived in another country or that a wife had gone to Spain and had been unfaithful *in that country* when she had never left the United States—have been held to be insane delusions.[8]

---

[7]Ingersoll v. Gourley, 78 Wash. 406.
[8]In re Kahn's Will, 5 N. Y. S. 556.

UNDUE INFLUENCE
OR DURESS

Undue influence or *duress* has been defined by the courts as that kind of mental or physical coercion that substitutes someone else's intentions in the will in place of the maker's desires. Stated in other language, undue influence consists of overpowering the maker's state of mind, without convincing the judgment. It is a question to be settled by a jury in a lawsuit between the relatives contesting the will and the beneficiary to whom a bequest was made.

There are no hard and fast requirements laid down by the courts as to when undue influence exists. More than mere argument, persuasion, or pleading must be involved. In cases where the claim of undue influence has been upheld, it is usually because the testator was in a weakened mental or physical state at the time the will was executed.[9]

Almost always, undue influence can be proved by resort to presumptions or by circumstantial evidence. Four cicumstances are usually said to be indications of undue influence by the courts.

1. The dispositions of property made in the will were not those that would normally be made to the natural heirs. At least a substantial part of the estate is left to "outsiders," rather than blood relatives who are the natural objects of the testator's bounty. This condition is not present, of course, when one blood relative gets a lion's share of the estate.

2. The testator was susceptible to domination or undue influence of others because of a weakened will or a weakened physical condition.

3. The individual claimed to have exerted undue influence had good opportunity to do so.

[9]In re Brown's Estate, 165 Ore, 575.

4. That individual had a disposition to influence the testator for financial gain, either personally or for the financial advantage of some associate or relative.

In the will contest involved in one New York case, a male testator left his fortune to another male with whom the testator had lived for a number of years. There was considerable evidence to show that this companion dominated the testator's life. When this case came up on appeal, the court said the question involved was whether the will "represented the intrinsic wishes and will of the testator, or was it the product of the command of the companion which the testator did not really want to follow, but was unable to resist." In this case, the Court of Appeals of New York held that a jury finding of undue influence was proper. The court commented:

> Where, as here, the record indicates that testator was pliable and easily taken advantage of, as [his companion] admitted, that there was a long and detailed history of dominance and subservience between them, that testator relied exclusively upon [his companion's] knowledge and judgment in the disposition of almost all of the material circumstances affecting the conduct of his life, and proponent [his companion] is willed virtually the entire estate, we consider that a question of fact was presented concerning whether the instrument offered for probate was the free, untrammeled and intelligent expression of the wishes and intentions of testator, or the product of the dominance of the beneficiary.[10]

The courts say that mere suspicion that undue influence was brought to bear is not sufficient. A bequest based entirely on kindness or affection, is proper, and undue influence is not necessarily physical injury or threat of it. It is a transaction or series of

[10]In re Kaufmann's Will, 257 N. Y. S. 2d 941, 205 N. E. 2d 864.

transactions that are ". . . the result of moral, social, or domestic force, conscientously and designedly exerted . . . and preventing true consent."[11]

What this seems to mean is that there is no clear-cut certainty about when property may be left to individuals who are not natural heirs. On the one hand, the courts say everyone has the right to dispose of property without restrictions. At the same time, other courts do not agree.

DISINHERITANCE OF A MISBEHAVING SPOUSE

As we have seen, some states have forced heirship laws, prohibiting disinheritance of a spouse. However, in the majority of these states this prohibition is not absolute. If a husband failed to support a wife, or if the wife abandoned the husband without real justification, the guilty spouse may not be able to claim an automatic statutory right to property when disinherited. But you cannot be certain that a faithless spouse may not show up to claim an inheritance that is otherwise considered an almost automatic right.

The fact that a husband and wife are living separately when one dies does not, standing alone, deprive the survivor of the right to make an election. A decree of divorce ends a marriage and also ends the right of either party to automatically inherit from the other. But the divorce decree must be final, rather than an interlocutory decree that is made final after the passage of a set period of time. If you can provide your executor with a court judgment or decree, holding that your spouse was guilty of misconduct, then it will be far easier to establish that the offending spouse is not entitled to inherit under the terms of state statutes.

[11]In re Null's Estate, 302 Pa. 64, 153 A. 139.

The burden of proof will be on your executor to prove misconduct on the part of the disinherited spouse, even though the facts may be undisputed at the time of the mistreatment. Therefore, in making your will, you should not rely on the executor's ability to justify the reason why the spouse was disinherited; proof should be supplied. It may also be advisable to make a statement in the will setting forth the reasons why the offending spouse was cut off. There is always a possibility that you may be living at some distance from the place where an abadonment occurred or from the locality where the husband or wife beat or mistreated the husband or wife to such an extent that he or she left. All this adds to the problems of proof.

This burden on the executor may come at a time when witnesses are difficult to locate. It should be remembered that the best witness to the mistreatment is usually the offended spouse, and unfortunately this witness will be deceased at the time of probate. Therefore, any available proof of misconduct should be left where it will be available to the executor.

5

Some Other Types of Wills

Actually, four different types of wills are used throughout the United States. The most common is the conventional, or so-called formal written will described in Chapter 4. The others are the holographic will, the oral or nuncupative will, and the mystic will. All states recognize the conventional written will, and some states permit the use of others, under controlled circumstances. Only Louisiana uses the mystic will.

HOLOGRAPHIC (SOMETIMES CALLED OLOGRAPHIC) WILLS

Approximately half the states in the United States recognize the use of a *holographic* or *olographic* will. These states, located principally in the south and west, are:

Alaska   North Dakota

Arizona   Oklahoma

Arkansas   Pennsylvania

California   South Dakota

Idaho   Tennessee

Kentucky   Texas

Louisiana   Utah

Mississippi   Virginia

Montana   West Virginia

Nevada   and Wyoming

North Carolina

The *holographic* will is a type that you actually write out
yourself. To be recognized as valid, it must be dated, written,
and signed entirely in the maker's own handwriting. No hand-
printed, typed, or printed material of any kind, even the month
of the year may be incorporated into it. In those states where a
holographic will is permitted, it is of equal validity with the
more commonly used formal, witnessed will. A holographic will
can be prepared with less formality than others because it does
not need to be witnessed. Since it is written entirely in the
handwriting of the testator, there is seldom any reason to believe
that it may have been forged. There is usually sufficient writing
to compare with samples of the testator's known handwriting;
but the requiring of witnesses for a conventional will performs a
valuable protective function. Not only do you have a lawyer who
is able to say that he drafted the will, but you have witnesses who
can testify that they actually saw the will executed, along with
the maker's signature on the document. Because of the absence of
protective ritual, these states that do recognize holographic wills
require very precise compliance with specific formalities.

A printed will form can never be used as part of a holographic will by filling in the appropriate blanks in the form. The requirement that the entire holographic will must be completely handwritten by the maker is absolute. Courts are unyielding on this requirement because the date, place and every other part of the entire document must be in the handwriting of the maker alone.[1]

If you should be searching for a will among the papers of a deceased relative or friend, do not overlook any paper that is wholly in the handwriting of the deceased. A letter or memorandum, which at first glance appears to be nothing other than a letter, may be recognized by the courts as a holographic will. Lawyers sometimes advise that a holographic will should never be written by an individual who is quite infirm or of extreme age. The general feeling of lawyers is that it is better to have the will executed before witnesses who can testify freely as to the maker's mental ability. As some persons reach advanced age, there may be a question concerning ability to draw up a plan for disposition of the estate or a question as to senility.

An additional potential drawback to a holographic will could arise if there is no one living who can readily identify the maker's handwriting.

NUNCUPATIVE OR ORAL WILLS

Historically, *nuncupative* or *oral* wills were first recognized by the courts as the right of a soldier or sailor anticipating death by going into battle. In some states, the right to make an oral will was eventually extended to persons in their last illness who

[1]In re Brooks Estate, 4 P. 2d 148, 214 Cal. 138.

had no opportunity to make a regular will. Where this right applies to non-military personnel, the law usually specifies that the maker must not only be in imminent peril of death but also actually die immediately thereafter. If the individual should escape death, the courts presume there would then be sufficient time for the maker to prepare a written will. One variety of an oral will is now recognized in more than half the states in the United States. But this right is usually recognized only under very limited circumstances.

Since this type of will permits an increased opportunity for fraud, it is looked on with disfavor by the courts and the lawmakers. Most jurisdictions require a will of this type to be reduced to writing and filed with a court within a specified period of from six days to six months after the declarations are made, and almost all states require the will to have been made before two or more competent witnesses.

Nothing but personal possessions of a maximum value of $30 to $1,000 may be disposed of by an oral will in some states. A few jurisdictions, however, place no limit on the type of property that may be disposed of, as well as no limit on the value, provided other statutory requirements are met. If there is any opportunity to make a conventional will, lawyers almost always advise that this be done in preference to a nuncupative will.

A MYSTIC WILL

A mystic will is used only in the state of Louisiana, although this is not the only type of will recognized in Louisiana. A *mystic will* is a closed and sealed document required by statute to be executed in a specific manner. It must be signed on the paper and on the outside of the envelope containing it, by a notary, by seven witnesses, and by the testator.[2]

[2]Civ. Code Louisiana, Article 1584.

DIFFERENCES BETWEEN A WILL, DEED, OR A CONTRACT

Sometimes it is not clear whether the writer of a document intended for it to be a will. The writing may have at least some of the requirements of a will, a deed, or a contract.

The test for a will stated by the courts is that the document or written instrument must express a genuine and clear present intent to dispose of property. If it appears to be a promise of future testamentary action—that is, to prepare a will in the future—then the courts will not interpret it as a will.[3] The basic idea is that:

> The court needs to be convinced that the statements of the transferor were deliberately intended to effectuate a transfer. People are often careless in conversation and in informal writings . . . Casual language, whether oral or written, is not intended to be legally operative . . .[4]

A will may usually be distinguished from a contract in several ways. The beneficiary of a will is not required to pay anything for the property or value received. The property is an outright gift. Under a contract, some value, recompense, or compensation, which is legally called *consideration,* must be given to the person who transfers property. A will, then, is a one-sided document. Legal rights do not exist when a will is made, coming into being when the maker dies. On the other hand, legal rights attach—become fixed or vested immediately at the time a contract is made.

In distinguishing a will from a deed, it is worth remember-

[3]Du Sauzay v. Du Sauzay, 63 So. 273, 105 Miss, 839.

[4]Gulliver and Tilson, "Classification of Gratuitous Transfers," 51 Yale Law Journal, 2–5, 1941.

ing that a will furnishes no present interest in property, and nothing passes under a will until the death of the maker. A deed passes a present interest in property, an interest that vests immediately. But under some deeds the right of use and enjoyment of the property may be postponed, although the ownership right comes into existence (that is, it is fixed (vests)) from the instant of the execution and delivery of the deed.

The moral of this is that your will should clearly state that it is a will. You should include language such as: "I, Richard Roundhouse Roe, of Long Beach, California, hereby make this my last will and testament, revoking every will heretofore made by me."

6

Getting Your Will Written

USING A LAYWER TO PLAN THE WILL

There are a number of reasons why it is advisable for a lawyer to plan your will with you. The lawyer's knowledge is the best guarantee that the necessary technical requirements will be met. Then too, most people are simply not aware of the interplay of legal relationships that may be involved. In addition, there is little likelihood that a will written by a lawyer will be ambiguous or indefinite.

One will written by a businessman without legal assistance illustrates what can happen. The testator wanted to divide his property equally between his two married children. His wife had died a short time before, and the testator had made the oldest child the beneficiary of his life insurance. In writing the will, the testator directed that half of his property was to go to each child. A lawyer could have pointed out that proceeds from the life insurance policy would go directly to the beneficiary and would not be handled by the executor of his will. Under the terms of the will, each child received half of the estate, excluding the life insurance policy. This, of course, worked an injustice on the younger child that the testator did not anticipate.

Selecting a Lawyer

Not wanting to admit that some lawyers are more qualified in some areas than others, the legal profession has made it difficult for the person on the street to find a lawyer well qualified for estate planning. While some lawyers may help you with estate plans, others may merely go through the motions of recording your instructions in legal language. Almost all of us select a lawyer with whom we communicate easily. By all means you want to have the feeling of being comfortable with your lawyer. The client should never feel inferior or intimidated. Legal problems are enough of a worry; you do not want to be under a personality strain while in the lawyer's office.

If your estate is of any size, you may want to consider a lawyer who specializes in estate planning and in drafting trust agreements, who has good knowledge of estate and income tax problems. Banks that handle trust matters will recommend a lawyer with this experience. Also, lawyers in the general practice of law can also direct you to experts. If there is a law school in your area, members of the faculty may also be knowledgeable about specialists in estate planning and legal tax matters.

Fees should be discussed with the lawyer at the time of the first visit, so there will be no misunderstanding of the costs involved. A flat fee may be charged for a comparatively simple will, with an hourly rate charged for drafting documents needed to handle a complicated situation.

In writing a will, a lawyer has nothing to sell but his or her time and skill in drafting documents that will protect you. It is the responsibility of you, the client, to make clear exactly what you want to accomplish with your property. The facts surrounding your personal and financial situation must therefore be explained in describing the objectives you want to achieve. You should give an accurate and fairly detailed picture of relationships and facts that may be significant, without describing side issues that take up unnecessary time. Remember that you pay for the lawyer's time. A lawyer's probing questions are not an attempt to pry into personal affairs. Such questions are part of a search for possible weak points in the document that the lawyer is drafting.

When an estate plan is set up, you must understand what the lawyer tells you at each step of the way. If the statements made to you are not clear, ask for additional explanation. Read each document drafted, and understand the reasons for provisions in the will or other legal papers. While lawyers approach a matter of this kind with considerable care, even the most prudent, cautious lawyer can make a mistake in inserting the wrong name of an individual in a document or in misinterpreting your desires concerning bequests. Make sure to proofread all papers yourself.

Information Your Lawyer Needs for the Estate Plan and for Drafting a Will

It has previously been pointed out that practically all lawyers draft wills, trusts, and other legal instruments on instructions of clients. But you may want to do more than have the lawyer stick to the bare bones request for a will.

The lawyer needs to know your aims and objectives, both for yourself and for your beneficiaries. It is not merely curiosity, but an attorney needs to know the extent of your estate and how you intend to handle it, both now and in your will. A client's plan to dispose of property, dictated to a lawyer for incorporation into a will, may turn out to be worthless—the entire estate may be eaten up by taxes or charges before half the bequests can be made. This may leave little or nothing for the widow and children, thus it is important for the lawyer to evaluate the extent of property and other assets, to make a rough estimate of the taxes, and to state how they will be paid.

At the minimum, your lawyer needs the following information in planning your will:

1. A list of real estate owned outright, with estimated value; any life estate that you own in other property; leases or rental agreements on property that you own, occupy or use, either as owner or tenant. The location of each individual property holding should be shown, as well as whether it is owned separately, owned with your spouse as joint tenants with right of survival, or owned as community property.

2. A record of all bank accounts owned jointly or individually, savings accounts, trust deeds, notes payable, stocks and bonds, and investment shares.

3. A list of personal items of exceptional value—jewelry, art objects, antique automobiles, and the like.

4. A list of all debts and obligations owned by you, including mortgages on your home or property.

5. A record of your life insurance policies, the annual premiums, the beneficiaries, and whether you can change beneficiaries, cash in polices, or make other changes.

6. A statement of value of any vested company retirement plans, annuities, or earned pension rights.

7. Detailed information about your immediate family, listing your spouse, living parents, and children. Details of any prior marriage, divorce decree, alimony, and children by a former wife should be listed. Stepchildren, adopted children, and illegitimate children should also be included.

8. Details concerning any business in which you are involved, if any, along with the interest owned by you. The approximate worth of this undertaking, income derived from it, and whether the business is a partnership, corporation, or association. Details concerning any arrangement to buy your interest in the event of death should also be listed.

9. Information about your spouse's style of living and anticipated income and needs.

10. A list of any inheritances expected by you or your spouse.

11. A statement concerning whether you have been given power to appoint (designate to whom certain family assets will pass upon your death) in family trusts or wills.

A check-off list of things to do immediately after the death of a loved one or friend appears in Appendix 2.

WHERE DO YOU KEEP YOUR WILL?

It is common to lock a will in a safe deposit box. This may be a mistake, since the safe deposit box may be sealed immediately after death by order of the state tax collector. If the safe deposit box is rented jointly with your spouse, the spouse may be able to gain entry, but there is no certainty that this will be allowed in a number of states. The end result is that insistence on storage in a safe place has made the will unavailable when it is needed most. But if the will is not stored in a safe place, it may be lost, deliberately destroyed, or subjected to tampering.

Some feel that if you have a lawyer, the best place to maintain the original of your will is in the lawyer's files. Individuals may hesitate to do this, since they do not use a lawyer with any frequency. But the lawyer who drafted it will usually be willing to maintain it in a lockbox with other wills the lawyer has drafted. Here again, if the lawyer does not have a fireproof safe or vault, the will may be subject to destruction. If you have named a bank as executor, or have set up a trust through bank facilities, then the original can usually be left at the bank.

Regardless of where the original is kept, it may be desirable to have a "conformed copy" among other papers that will be readily available to relatives who will look into your personal matters shortly after death. A *conformed copy* is an exact copy of the will that has your written signature replaced by a typed notation: signed by_____(your name)_____ on_____(date)_____ . And even though a conformed copy may be available in your papers, it is desirable for a close relative or trusted friend to know exactly where your will is maintained.

RECORD KEEPING
BEYOND YOUR WILL

Your survivors should not have to conduct an exhaustive search to learn what property you owned and what should be done with it. Experience shows that a letter of instructions, left in addition to your will, can be very helpful to family members in closing your affairs. This letter does not need to be a formal document, without typing errors, and it is generally not necessary to have the aid of a lawyer in preparing this information. But it should include enough detail to enable your family to locate confidential bank accounts, life insurance policies, survivor's benefits, or simply family momentos that you want to pass on. Some letters of this kind also include requests about the kind of funeral or memorial arrangements desired.

While a letter of instructions has no legal force, it should not be in conflict with the terms of your will. If there is any question, the will should be reviewed when your letter of instructions is written. It may also be desirable to clearly state that the letter is in no way intended to replace your existing will or to be construed as a new will. After completion, it is suggested that the letter of instructions be maintained alongside your will in a safe and confidential place. Like your will, it may contain financial information that you do not want commonly known.

Since you will have no opportunity to explain the contents of a letter of this kind, it should be understandable to a complete stranger. The contents should be in such detail that all vital addresses, names, descriptions, and other information is self-explanatory. It is suggested that this letter include some or all of the following:

1. *Details about insurance and survivor's benefits.* A list of all life insurance policies owned and their locations should include any life insurance coverage at your place of employment or business, as well as personal or fraternal association insurance. Eligibility for Social Security and/or veteran's benefits should also be set out in detail.

2. *A list of bank accounts.* This should include both checking and savings accounts, by name and address of the bank and by account number. A statement as to where your old bank statements and cancelled checks are stored may also be helpful. This will be of value in the preparation of tax returns.

3. *Identification of any safe deposit boxes rented.* State where the key is stored and who has access. Also briefly list any items of unusual value in the box.

4. *A list of important personal documents.* Show the location of important personal papers, especially those that may be needed to prove birth, Social Security numbers, marriage, or divorce. Such information may be vital in establishing claims for insurance or death benefits. Location of automobile registration papers should also be included.

5. *A list of accounts receivable.* A list of all monies, promissory notes, or sums owed to you, along with how these obligations by others can be proved.

6. *A record of time payments as well as other debts that you are obligated to pay.*

7. *A copy of house and mortgage records.* This includes deeds, title insurance, tax payment records, and other papers pertaining to home ownership.

8. *Location of personal income tax returns, both state and federal.*

9. *A list of investments, stock brokerage accounts, and the location of securities.* The price paid for each stock or security should be available.

10. *A list of current credit cards, by number.*

11. *Names and addresses of persons to be notified of funeral arrangements, in the event they desire to attend.* This may include any details you want to set out about the type of service and how it should be conducted. A family representative should be requested to obtain ten copies of the death certificate from the funeral director. These certificates will be helpful in filing claims for insurance and survivor's benefits.

12. *A list of professional and business contacts to be notified.* At the minimum, this should include your insurance agent, tax accountant, employer, lawyer, and executor.

ADDITIONAL RECORD KEEPING TO SAVE YOUR HEIRS' MONEY

Few of us want to be bothered with record keeping that is not required by law or that is not absolutely essential. But there are simple, practical steps that almost anyone can take to shelter part of that person's estate from unnecessary taxes. If you owned a house or condominium, for example, you can begin by making a written record of permanent improvements that have been made over the years, itemizing costs of each outlay. Without cancelled checks or receipts, twenty years from now your children might not be able to prove that you spent $1,000 for the improvements that went into your home or condominium.

A record of such expenditures will ease the flow of the capital gains tax when your home is eventually sold by the executor of the estate.

GETTING RID OF QUESTIONABLE ODDS AND ENDS OF STOCK

Over the years, some investors have accumulated small lots of worthless stock, as well as odd batches of a share or two that have been received as stock splits or other transactions. Realizing that someone may take over the management of your affairs, you should consider liquidating or consolidating such odds and ends. Frequently the value represented by these accumulations is small, but they would cause an executor a number of headaches. Therefore, it may be advisable to junk worthless items, to consolidate odd lots, and to sell off those stocks that are no longer listed on the stock market.

ESCHEAT PROBLEMS (WHEN THE STATE INHERITS PROPERTY)

Escheat is the legal name given to this process by which the state gains ownership. A basic rule of property law is that ownership reverts to the state if heirs cannot be found following the death of the property owner. There are some differences in escheat laws from state to state, but they uniformly provide that if an owner of unclaimed money or property has no contact with the money or property for a specified number of years, the property is considered as abandoned. And all abandoned property is owned by the state in which the property lies.

Laws of this kind, which are sometimes called *unclaimed* or *abandoned property statutes,* bring large sums of money into state treasuries every year. If the owner of real estate pays taxes on the property, the state has sufficient contact with the owner. But sometimes a bank account shows no activity for several years. After a specified number of years of inactivity, the account is turned over to the state. Banks, savings and loans, and other financial institutions send out written notices well in advance of the statutory limit.

Some of these bank accounts have undoubtedly been secretly maintained, while others were opened by individuals living alone, who may have died suddenly or by accident. Most of these unclaimed bank accounts contain relatively small balances— amounts like $25, $400, or up to $1,000. But some individual unclaimed accounts may include very large sums. New York state, for example, recently reported that $265 million was collected in the thirty-one years that escheat laws had been in operation in that state, with only 12 percent of that total being returned to heirs who were eventually able to uncover the existence of accounts and to establish rightful ownership. In a single year recently, the state of Massachusetts collected $647,393 in escheat monies.

The well-known entertainer, W. C. Fields, was so concerned with dying penniless that he secreted funds under fictitious names in two hundred different banks in cities all around the United States. On Fields' death in 1946, only forty-five of these two hundred secret accounts were ever found and claimed. An estimated $600,000 in hidden money was never located by his heirs.

The contents of abandoned safe deposit boxes are also turned over to the state, after the box rent has not been paid for a specified period of time. If neither the person renting the box nor heirs come forward, state tax officials take any cash in the box and auction off any other property found therein. Gold coins, jewelry, heirlooms, and similar items go to the highest bidder. Personal and family treasures and mementos are thrown away, unless they are sold at the auction.

It is not necessary for anyone to have much detailed knowledge of escheat laws, if we keep workable records of our property. It is a good idea to list all savings accounts, bank books, and safe deposit boxes in your letter of instructions to your heirs, even though you may not want to write a will. Some individuals simply have no heirs. Escheat of their property can be prevented by writing a will leaving property to a charity, friends, or others rather than let it go to the state.

WHICH STATE LAW CONTROLS?

If there is no will, personal property is disposed of under the terms of state inheritance laws, such as the laws of devise and descent, at the place of the deceased's domicile or legal residence. Real estate is disposed of under the terms of the state law where the land or property is located.

A will must be valid under the requirements of the state law where it is submitted for probate. It is therefore extremely important to consider revising your will if you move from state to state. If, for example, you are relying on a holographic will written when living in California, you would die intestate if you took your property and moved to a state like New York, where a holographic will is not recognized.

Writing Your Own Will   *69*

Individuals frequently write their own will, without legal assistance. And there are times when a homemade will may be adequate in all respects. But there are a number of serious risks in attempting to write your own will.

In the first place, an estate that has been carefully accumulated over a lifetime deserves to be disposed of by a document that has been written to anticipate unforeseen contingencies and problems that may arise. If carefully drawn by a lawyer, it will incorporate those precise terms and legal ideas that have been tested over many years, which cover problems not apparent to the layperson. Your will should be drafted to your individual situation—considering family needs and potential problems.

If both lawyer and client devote the time to it, the lawyer may help considerably in estate planning. If the will is drawn to accommodate individual needs, there may be some possible options of which you are not aware. The lawyer may suggest the use of a trust to accomplish certain purposes. In addition, the lawyer may be able to reduce the taxes that your heirs will eventually be forced to pay in estate taxes, capital gains taxes, or state inheritance levies.

Then too, the best assurance that your will meets all the legal requirements is to have it prepared by a lawyer. You simply may not use the proper terms or legal expressions. Language that may be adequate in everyday affairs may simply not satisfy the courts. The lawyer not only knows how to reduce the likelihood that a will may be challenged or broken but is also trained to cut out inconsistencies or ambiguities in wording that could cause serious difficulties when the will comes up for probate. All in all, it is desirable to have your will drafted by a professional, preferably a lawyer who handles estate planning.

THE PREPRINTED WILL FORM

Preprinted will forms, with blanks to be filled in by the maker, are available at stationery stores in many states. A form of this kind is seen in Appendix 3. In the first place, these will forms may never be revised by the printing house that made them up, regardless of how long they stay on the market. Tax laws, especially the federal requirements, frequently change, and there is always a possibility that you are using a form that is less advantageous from a tax standpoint. While it is not very likely, there is always a chance that the form does not comply with state law requirements. But the likelihood of a problem may be increased considerably if you picked up the form in one state and used it when you wrote a will in another.

Further, a serious objection to the use of these forms is that they are often too rigid. It is simply not possible to print all the widely varying needs of different people into one will form, or even into several variations of it. The user generally has only one choice where options should be available. Persons who have used these forms have also pointed out that it is rather easy to misinterpret the instructions or to fail to anticipate answers needed to fill in the blanks. If you write in some changes to suit your own needs, changing the wording of the preprinted blank, you may unintentionally change the legal meaning. Will forms are simply not authoritative—they have value only as suggestions.

It is also worth pointing out again that you cannot use a preprinted will form to write a holographic will. The courts quite uniformly reject this notion, since such a will was not prepared "wholly in the handwriting of the testator," as required for any holographic will.

7

Other Provisions That May Be Included In Your Will

There is no set formula concerning the wording of a will. But some items, other than major bequests, should be considered.

It is human nature that wives should regard household furniture and furnishings as their own. To avoid any problem in this regard, it may be advisable for the husband's will to contain a recitation that all furniture, furnishings, silver, china, crystal, and all other household effects are the separate property of the wife, or are granted to her.

If historic family photographs, the family tea set, heirlooms, the antique sideboard, or other items of this nature are being passed along by a will to family members, give consideration to leaving a life estate, rather than an outright grant. This means that when the recipient of the life estate dies, the property must be passed on to a named individual or class of individuals, such as grandchildren. This technique should serve to keep items of sentimental value in the family.

HAVING TAXES ON LEGACIES PAID OUT OF THE RESIDUE OF THE ESTATE

If the maker of a will included a bequest of $10,000 to a certain individual, then undoubtedly the maker intended for that beneficiary to receive $10,000. But there are times when it does not work out that way. In order to distribute the estate tax, the executor may withhold a proportionate share from specific legacies. This withholding can be avoided by the testator, however, if the will specifically directs that bequests shall be tax-free, with all taxes to be made from the residuary estate. Consideration may be given to inclusion of a clause of this type in any will.

A survey of a large number of wills offered for probate in 1978 reflected that less than one-fourth of the wills filed made any mention of payment of estate taxes or inheritance taxes from funds of the deceased's estate. Apparently, this possibility is never called to the attention of the testator in many instances.

ESTATE APPRAISERS

In most states laws require the probate court to appoint appraisers. Then the administrator's or executor's responsibility is to see that proper appraisal statements are filed with the court. From the standpoint of a creditor, these appraisals may be desirable. But from the deceased's standpoint these appraisals may be an unnecessary expense. Some states do not require an appraisal if the will states that this formality may be dispensed with. Actual experience shows that these appraisal statements or settlements are frequently not audited in any event.

GRANTING AUTHORITY TO SELL, BORROW, OR MORTGAGE THE ESTATE

An executor has authority to sell, exchange, borrow, or mortgage real estate only as authorized by the will or by an order of the probate court. It may be very advantageous to sell property immediately, if a "once in a lifetime" offer should be made to the executor. But permission from the probate court may be a long time in coming or may never be granted. In some instances, permission to sell may be held up indefinitely because the probate judge—not familiar with the property or with surrounding real estate values—is reluctant to approve. This potential hardship on the estate can be avoided by a statement in the will giving the executor authority to meet payments on the home mortgage, to pay tax bills, to sell property, to exchange, mortgage, or borrow on any estate property. This kind of provision in a will is especially helpful to the estate in situations where property or individual assets may be declining in value.

It may also be advisable to give the executor specific authority to file a joint income tax return with the surviving wife or husband. This authority should include the right to exercise any options or rights the deceased had available under the Internal Revenue Code.

Another matter to consider is that of leaving the executor some liquid assets. When the estate owes a heavy tax bill, all available liquid assets may not total enough to satisfy the bill. Frequently, the estate may have considerable value, but the executor can do little to free assets unless given the power by a specific provision in the will. It is also desirable to have enough liquidity for the executor to make regular payments on a widow's or widower's allowance, pending settlement.

It it appears likely that the executor may be short of cash, provisions may be included in the will for the executor to make distribution of assets or property in kind. If the deceased left sixty shares of Union Pacific stock and there were four heirs, then the executor could distribute fifteen shares to each heir. A provision of this kind in a will would also permit distribution of stock in a family-owned corporation, avoiding the possibility that family control might be lost through a forced sale. Life insurance, of course, is generally the best estate tool to assure that your executor will have sufficient liquid assets to take care of immediate problems.

CONTINUING THE FAMILY BUSINESS

A business that is a thriving enterprise while the owner is alive may be practically worthless without the dynamic presence of the founder. For example, the owner of a hardware store in a moderate-sized midwestern town said nothing in his will about the continuance of his business. He neglected to give authority to his executor in the will. Since the executor could not replace hardware stock items in the store as it was sold off, regular customers started to go elsewhere for their needs. By the time the probate court had finally granted authority to the executor, the business, which was built up over a lifetime, had dried up.

Death of the owner or operator of a firm may cause two basic problems:

1. hindering continued operation, or

2. getting true value from sale of the business.

As a matter of law, an executor has neither the authority nor the legal duty to carry on any business in which the decedent was engaged. If the executor does so without authority from the will or without prior probate court approval, the executor will be held personally liable for any losses sustained in the operation of the business. This liability on the executor is absolute, whether or not the executor used good judgment in operating this firm. This is over and above the fact that the executor continues to be personally accountable for any profits made.

Authority for the executor to continue the deceased's business may be conferred by a provision in the will. It may also be granted by the express written consent of all heirs, beneficiaries, and any other individuals who may have any interest in the estate. Sometimes all of these parties in interest will not give permission, and it may be a time-consuming agreement to work out. Experience shows, therefore, that it is preferable to include authority in the will. It is also suggested that the will specify whether the executor is to continue the business, to wind up the business, or to allow the decision to be made in accordance with the business judgment of the executor. Some businesses, of course, are readily marketable. Others may be difficult to sell at a price anywhere near real value, owing to the unusual contributions made by the deceased owner or partner. To cover situations of this kind, owners or partners sometimes have a written buy-and-sell agreement between themselves, contracting for the survivors to buy the business from heirs of an owner who dies.

One workable arrangement of this kind is an agreement binding the surviving owners or partners to sell under a price agreement incorporated into a contract. A selling price of this kind may vary from year to year, based on a previously agreed on figure, or on an appraisal made by an outside individual or firm on a specified date each year. If the business interests are sizeable, the buy-and-sell agreement may call for payment in installments. Some businesses circumvent this problem by insuring the life of each of the partners or owners, by buying an insurance policy equal to the purchase price that must be paid for the deceased's interest.

In some instances, of course, it may be advisable to incorporate a family business, even though the company may be essentially owned and managed by the head of the family. Stock can then be left by will to one or more family members, or left as part of a trust for the benefit of the wife and other children who have no interest or background in the operation of the business.

LEAVING BODY ORGANS FOR TRANSPLANT

You may also want to consider leaving your eyes, kidneys, heart, or other organs to someone in critical need of a transplant. This may be done in your will, but of course the organs would be worthless as transplants by the time your will could be probated.

In a number of states, an automobile driver's license contains a space for written authorization for donation of body parts for transplants. This authorization is to cover the eventuality that an organ could be taken immediately should the holder of the license be killed in an accident. A typical attachment of this kind for the reverse side of a driver's license appears in Appendix 4.

The National Kidney Foundation, 116 East 27th Street, New York, New York 10016, will make available a form giving authorization for the donation of transplantable organs. This form is considered legally valid in all fifty states.

If your will should include a bequest of all or part of your body for educational or scientific purposes, you should have a written understanding with members of your immediate family and/or doctor. This, of course, is because of the short time that organs are transferable after death. A neighborhood research hospital or the nearest medical school generally has printed forms giving a hospital or other institution authority to use your body for research or to transplant an organ.

A SO-CALLED LIVING WILL

A so-called *living will* is not a will at all. It is simply a formal written request to be allowed to die, after it is obvious that survival can only be sustained by continued use of mechanical and artificial means. Most of us, of course, want to enjoy life to the end. But to many people, it seems pointless to continue living when there is no meaningful existence—when remaining alive is possible only by use of a heart-lung machine, intravenous feedings, and the application of other life support devices.

An example of a living will, that you may write for yourself, is set out in Appendix 5.

SIMULTANEOUS DEATH OF HUSBAND AND WIFE

No person inherits property upon the death of another unless the survivor lives an instant longer than the decedent. With the coming of the automobile and the airplane, it became increasingly difficult to tell whether the husband or wife died first in an accident. This determination is often important in the settlement of the husband's and wife's property, since all or part of the estate may go to whoever survived longer.

To take care of this problem, all but four states have passed a law called the *Uniform Simultaneous Death Act,* or a law that accomplishes the same purpose. These laws all provide that if it cannot be determined which of the two spouses died first, the property of each spouse shall be disposed of as if that individual had survived the other. If both the husband and wife are joint tenants with the right of survivorship, one-half of the property so owned would be distributed as if one tenant survived, and the other half would be distributed as if the other tenant survived. This act applies to the proceeds of a life insurance policy, to property left by will, or to property of a person who died without a will.

One of the effects of the *Uniform Simultaneous Death Act* is that one parent's property will pass down his or her family line, rather than to the heirs of a spouse who survived for a moment or two longer than his or her mate. This law also avoids the possibility of double taxation, as well as the costs of double estate administration over the same assets in quick succession.

In almost all states where the *Simultaneous Death Act* or similar law is in force, a declaration may be made in a will to the effect that the wife shall be deemed to have survived the husband. This provision permits a claim to be made for a marital deduction, which may result in a considerable saving on the federal estate tax in the event of the simultaneous deaths of both husband and wife. How the marital deduction affects the tax picture is described in a subsequent chapter. If the marital deduction is not in keeping with the general scheme of the couple's estate plan, it may be advantageous to have a declaration in the wife's will that the husband shall be deemed to have survived last.

8

Rewriting
Your Will

The last will that one writes is the only will that counts, because the last valid instrument does away with the others, if the will so states.

You should look at your will from time to time, with the thought of revision in mind. It is, of course, possible to prepare a legal *codicil,* which is an addition or change to your will. But it may be preferable to have the entire will rewritten, especially if there is any chance that the terms of the will may be confused by a codicil. No piece of planning is good forever. What is right for a person at one time of life may not be appropriate a few years later.

The history of the entire western world might have been

different if Julius Caesar had taken the time to change his will after fathering a son by Cleopatra. Instead, Caesar's will named his grandnephew Octavian, who later became the Emperor Augustus, as his political and family heir. This gave Octavian the political and financial start he needed to become the first Roman emperor.

When one of your beneficiaries either marries or dies, there may be good reason to revise your will. Also, a new will is usually a must after going through a divorce. You should remember that you cannot write in changes in your old instrument without running the risk of having the entire will or at least some of its major provisions declared invalid at the time of probate.

Then too, both federal and state tax laws may change. For example, new requirements and provisions in the *Federal Tax Reform Act of 1976* made it advisable for many persons to consider such changes. Some of the changes in the *Reform Act of 1976* will not become fully operative until 1981.

RE-EXAMINING YOUR WILL IN LIGHT OF CHANGED TAX PROVISIONS

If your will was written before 1976, it may be advisable to review the will with your attorney, because of changes in the federal tax and gift laws. New provisions that could be applicable to your particular situation were passed in 1976 and 1977, but some will not take effect until 1981. For example, in 1976 a new marital deduction rule was passed into law, permitting you to leave half of your adjusted gross estate, or $250,000, whichever is larger, to your spouse tax-free. This change in the marital deduction may have crucial application to many estates of moderate size, especially those in the $150,000-to-$500,000 class.

Prior to 1977, lawyers almost uniformly drafted wills to give the surviving spouse the maximum marital deduction permitted by law. This was usually advantageous from a tax standpoint at the time, but it may not be so under the revised marital deduction. How this works out in practice is set out in the section on the marital deduction, in Chapter 16.

CHANGING YOUR WILL IF YOU MOVE TO ANOTHER STATE

Americans tend to be quite mobile. One reason is that businesses frequently transfer employees from state to state. You should consider revising your will not only to change your property's distribution, but you should also consider a revision whenever you change your residence to another state. Legal requirements controlling the use of wills may be different. For example, a holographic will made in the first state may not be recognized in the second. Legal requirements for a formal will may also be different. Then too, one state may follow the old common law ideas of property ownership, while the new state may be a community property state. And there are still differences in two common law states or two community property jurisdictions.

Even if the will made in the old place of residence is still recognized by the courts where you move, you may nevertheless have problems. When your will is offered for probate, the usual procedure is for the probate judge to have it proved by the testimony of at least one witness. To do this, the witness must appear before the probate authorities and swear that the will was executed in his or her presence. To pay the expenses for a witness to come to California from Maine can involve needless expense and delay. This problem would be avoided by a new will made before local witnesses at the new place of domicile.

An executor appointed by a will made in one state may be legally unqualified to serve in another state. In a number of jurisdictions, only residents of the state in which the will is probated are legally qualified to serve as executors. Then too, if a bank has been named as executor, it should be pointed out that the bank's charter usually permits it to conduct business only in the state or states where the bank is located.

When the deceased owned property in two states, it may be necessary to have a second administration, called an *ancillary administration,* conducted in the state away from the state of residence. If you own a beach cottage or mountain cabin in another state, officials in the latter state may claim that you were a legal resident of that latter state, attempting to force your heirs to pay state inheritance or estate taxes in that state as well as the state where you actually reside. While this secondary claim can usually be defeated, it can prove troublesome. Situations of this kind can usually be avoided by your attorney, provided your attorney is aware of the potential problem in advance. The legal techniques used to avoid this ancillary administration may vary, depending on the laws on the two states involved. One way to avoid this ancillary administration would be to place the property located in the second state in a revocable trust. (Revocable trusts are studied in Chapters 15 and 17.)

Another way to avoid the ancillary administration would be to have the property owned jointly by the husband and wife, with right of survivorship in a life estate. After the termination of the life estate, the property would be owned outright by the couple's children. The life estate would, of course, permit the husband and wife to use the property during their lifetime, as long as they did not harm the *corpus,* which is the substance of the property. Harming the property would mean tearing down buildings or other destructive acts.

A CODICIL TO A WILL

A *codicil* is a supplement to a will. Its purpose is to change, enlarge, or in some way clarify the terms of an existing will.

In many instances a will may be revised by a codicil, rather than by rewriting the entire instrument. A codicil cannot serve as a will, in and by itself. Neither is it a new or an after-made will. Consequently, a codicil is dependent for its legal force on the will which it supplements. A codicil to a will must be executed with exactly the same legal formalities as were required of the original will. Otherwise, the codicil portion is not valid.[1]

Frequently, the testator may turn to a codicil, feeling that a change in his or her will is necessary. But the use of the codicil is not always the best procedure. After a codicil or two has been added, there is an increased likelihood that the changes create the possibility of misinterpretation or outright conflict about what the maker intended. Frequently, the best way is to draft a new will at this stage, with clear-cut provisions.

REVOCATION (CANCELLATION) OF AN EXISTING WILL

One of the legal problems frequently in the courts is to determine which of two wills is valid. When a new will is prepared, the old will should be revoked. That is why most new wills have a statement in the introductory part of the document to the effect that "this will revokes all other wills previously written by me." Normally, the date on the last will written prevails. While not likely, there is always a chance that a writing

---

[1]Paul v. Davenport, 7 S. E. 2d 352, 217 N. C. 154.

intended to operate as a will could be construed as a codicil to a prior will. And if prior wills are not revoked, there is always the possibility that one of them could be presented for probate, unless it is clear that his prior will had been cancelled.

A specific statement of revocation is perhaps the best way to cancel a prior will. Usually, the maker cancels a prior will by writing a new one, with some different bequests. In rare instances, however, an individual who has previously written a will decides he or she wants to die intestate. Usually, this can be done by destroying all wills that the individual may have written in the past. Most states, however, now have statutes that permit you to write a will, revoking prior wills, but making no disposition of your estate in the latter document. The courts here interpret this to mean that the maker has died intestate.[2]

At any rate, the maker of a will should not merely strike through some portion of it, believing that part of the entire document had been cancelled. If the maker wants to revoke the will by damaging it, the act must be such that there is deliberate damage to some basic part of the writing, not merely the edge of the paper. If the maker really wants to revoke it in this manner, it is best to tear the will to bits and destroy all pieces.[3]

The courts have held that the maker of a will may revoke it by burning, and that this may be accomplished by a burning of the document itself, not merely burning the envelope or outside cover that contained the will.[4] The safest method is to write a new will, stating that the new will revokes all others, and then to destroy the old will and all copies, so completely that someone could never submit the unwanted will for probate. *Destruction of the original will may not be enough:* All existing copies should also be destroyed. Otherwise, a beneficiary under this will could get one of the copies admitted to probate by claiming that the origi-

[2]Grotts v. Casburn, 295 Ill. 286, 3 A. L. R. 836.
[3]Crampton v. Osborn, 356 Mo. 125.
[4]White v. Casten, 46 N. C. 197.

nal had been burned in an accidental fire and that the copy was therefore valid.

REVOCATION BY OPERATION OF THE LAW

In a number of states, a valid will may be automatically revoked by operation of law when there are specific changes in the maker's family relationships. For example, a single man may have a perfectly valid will. However, it may be revoked by the terms of state law if he should marry. The idea here is that the new wife should be provided for and that, if the husband does not write a new will, then the wife will automatically be provided for as an heir of an intestate husband.

In some states this old principle of automatic revocation has been done away with by statute, but in certain other states, this old English common law idea still prevails. In some other states the entire will may not be revoked, but it would include a newborn child as an automatic heir to a percentage of the estate.

In those states where there could be an automatic revocation of a will, it does not come into place except in instances of marriage, divorce, birth of a child, or death of a principal beneficiary. A lawyer should be consulted for individual differences in state laws pertaining to automatic revocation and for the steps that should be taken to keep a valid will in force.

9
Probate

For every thousand persons dying each year in the United States, fewer than five hundred administrations are filed with the probate courts. This includes administrations for persons leaving a will, as well as for those dying intestate. What this means is that in well over 50 percent of deaths:

1. court administration has simply never been needed by surviving family members, due to the small size of the estate, or

2. the survivor's family is able to pay off debts and reach an amicable settlement for the distribution of property on its own.

If the estate is small in value, it may be settled without a formal court administration. Some states have statutes that allow the transfer of title to an automobile, simply on an affidavit from the heirs. In still other states, the county clerk or another designated official can issue an affidavit in lieu of probate, declaring who is entitled to property in a small estate. In other jurisdictions, a court hearing can be held to permit a property settlement, to transfer a small amount of stock, or to handle the collection or payment of the debts of a deceased.

If the estate is of more than minimum size, however, it must go through the administration process set up by state laws. *Probate* is the legal process through which the courts officially designate a document as the legally acceptable, property prepared, and correctly executed will of the decedent. From the viewpoint of the courts, an instrument is not actually a will until it is presented and the proper court "proves out" the instrument by ruling that it is legal under applicable state laws. The purported will must be found to be such in reality. In most states a *written instrument,* which is a purported will, may be offered for probate by any individual who has a possible financial interest in the estate—the executor, an heir, a beneficiary, or any person who may have a claim against the deceased. The term "probate" is also used to mean the settlement or disposition of any kind of an estate before the courts—either a disposition under a will or an estate where the deceased died intestate.

SHOULD PROBATE BE AVOIDED AT ALL COST?

In recent years a number of commonly read publications have urged the public to avoid probate at all costs. There is no question that probate costs money, and that under this procedure assets may be tied up. But avoidance of probate should seldom be the only goal of estate planning. If the estate is small or if the estate is made up of jointly owned property, the process may be unnecessary. And if the property passes under the terms of a trust, then probate may be avoided. But the avoidance of probate, merely to eliminate the probate fees, may not be desirable at all, considering the overall objectives of the estate.

PROBATE PROCEDURES

Required procedures for proving due or proper execution of a will vary considerably from state to state. In some jurisdictions, two attesting witnesses must come into court and give testimony that the instrument is genuine and was properly prepared and witnessed.

Some other states require the appearance and testimony of only one attesting witness, with some jurisdictions allowing this one witness to give a deposition, rather than to be required to appear in court in person. Should all witnesses be dead at the time the will is offered for probate, proper execution may be proved by two witnesses to the handwriting of any of the signatures, either signature of the testator or that of any witness. A number of states have adopted a legal procedure for the use of so-called *self-proving wills.* This involves a procedure by which both the testator and the witnesses to a will execute a sworn affidavit at the time the will is made, swearing that all the legal requirements for due execution were complied with. Later, when the testator dies and the purported will is offered for probate, this affidavit is accepted as proof instead of requiring testimony in person before the probate court.

Some states have statutes requiring the individual appointed as executor in someone else's will to bring the will in for probate within thirty days after the death of the testator. The individual appointed as executor is subject to a fine or jail sentence for failing to bring in the will, but the executor must have knowledge of the death of the testator before such a penalty may apply.

Previously, we have stressed the fact that witnesses to a will should preferably be established residents of the community who are likely to continue to live in that area. It is also important to select witnesses who are likely to outlive the testator. If witnesses are deceased at the time the will is offered for probate, it may be difficult to prove the authenticity of the will, simply because there may be no one who can testify to the execution of that will. And if the witnesses have moved far away, the court costs in transporting witnesses back to the probate hearing may be considerable.

As noted earlier, in recent years some writers have gained public attention by urging everyone to avoid probate if at all possible. This is because the preparation of legal forms and papers is almost always necessary during the time of the probate procedure. Legal charges for this kind of work may consume from 1 to 10 percent of the value of the estate. Probate may also be disadvantageous for heirs to an estate, since they are required to wait while the estate is settled through the machinery of the probate process. Heirs usually feel entitled to their bequest without any delay.

Of course, not all property goes through probate. The proceeds from most types of life insurance policies are paid directly to the heirs, avoiding probate. Somewhat similarly, if property is owned by joint tenants with the right of survivorship, the ownership of such property passes automatically to the survivor. Depending on state laws, jointly owned stocks and bank accounts may also avoid probate. Certain trust arrangements may also be used to avoid the costs and delays of probate.

While you may want to minimize the amount of assets that must be disposed of by will through probate, it is not always advantageous to avoid the procedure. For one thing, passing property through the probate procedure generally lets family members know what was intended by the testator, putting a stop to family disputes before they can arise. Probate has a legal finality, and this frequently cuts down the likelihood that assets will be dissipated through bitter family quarrels. In the final analysis, the decision concerning which specific properties or assets should be kept out of probate should rest with the individual and his or her estate planner and adviser on tax costs. A typical Probate of Will Check Sheet appears in Appendix 6.

THE EXECUTOR OR EXECUTRIX

A well drawn will may not always achieve intended results unless handling of the estate is entrusted to the right person. The importance of selecting this proper individual as executor or executrix should therefore be emphasized. This same attention should also be given to selecting someone, such as a trustee, to handle a trust for you.

Ideally, the individual chosen as executor or executrix should not only have the decedent's best interests at heart but should also have some reasonable background in business, finance, and matters of the world. But regardless of experience, the executor may need access to an attorney, in order to draw up necessary legal papers for court and give legal advice. The executor or executrix may obtain this legal help, along with that of other professionals such as real estate appraisers or tax accountants, with the approval of the probate court. Their professional fees may be charged to the estate.

Executors may not charge any fees, but this is most unusual. In some instances they may waive their fees and serve out of family obligation. Almost always, however, the executor is fully deserving of whatever pay is received. Commissions or fees are usually set by state law.

The following case illustrates what may happen if the executor is concerned with selfish interests rather than with preserving assets and handling affairs of the estate. A European businessman came to the United States as a refugee when Nazi troops swept over a large part of Europe. The businessman's only son was also expected to leave Nazi territory a short time later. But the son got caught up in the political and military turmoil of the times. The son's exact whereabouts were known for a time, but eventually he disappeared. About this time the father died in the United States, leaving a substantial amount of money in a trust set up by will. Under the terms of the will and the trust agreement, an acquaintance was appointed to settle the estate and to serve as trustee for the father's trust. The executor was instructed by the deceased to take all reasonable and logical steps to find the son and to turn the substance of the trust over to him. If this could not be done, the funds in the trust were to be given to a distant relative of the father. Year after year, the executor-trustee diligently sought out the missing son in the bistros, nightclubs, and hotels in Europe. This search went on and on, in London, Paris, Rome, Athens, and resorts along the Italian and French Riviera. Eventually, the executor-trustee got tired of traveling, and most of the estate assets had been dissipated. Legally, perhaps the executor-trustee could justify his actions as stipulated in the will and trust agreement. But this was not quite the handling of the estate that the father had intended.

A RELATIVE AS EXECUTOR OR EXECUTRIX

It is apparent that any executor or executrix has a time-consuming job, requiring continuing integrity. In some respects, a surviving wife or husband may be the logical person to serve as executor or executrix of the estate of the other. Since the bulk of a couple's property is usually left to the surviving spouse, no one else may be so interested as the survivor in protecting estate assets.

But frequently there are drawbacks in appointing a surviving spouse to handle an estate. Sometimes the survivor is so emotionally involved that affairs may not be concluded to best advantage. Then too, the surviving spouse may not actually have sufficient knowledge of business or legal affairs. This is sometimes especially true if a surviving wife has not had a career of her own, and has actually been out of close contact with business and financial affairs. One solution is to name a knowledgeable son or daughter as co-executor with the surviving wife. Another solution is to name the family lawyer as co-executor along with the surviving wife. The attorney can devote a minimum of time preparing or checking the preparation of paperwork and guiding the surviving wife in avoiding business and financial troubles. Most of the actual handling of estate matters could be handled by the wife.

Legal authority for a relative to serve as an executor is sometimes a problem. In the majority of states, a non-resident son or daughter who is designated as executor or executrix may not only be legally required to designate a process agent to receive legal papers and summons but may also be required to post a bond.

USING A TRUST COMPANY OR TRUST DEPARTMENT OF A BANK

If the estate is small, a trust company or bank may not agree to serve as executor of an estate. A close relative or friend may serve without charge. At the same time, the relative may be more sympathetic to the testator's wishes, personal problems, and financial condition. Nevertheless, an executor from an outside bank or trust company is less likely to become emotionally involved. In addition, the personal representative you have chosen may die, leaving your estate without direction unless you designate an alternate. For consistent dependability, it may be best to designate a trust company or the trust department of a full service bank. Should the estate be complicated or subject to family squabbles, it may ultimately be less expensive to have the duties performed by such an outside firm. Then too, a bank or trust company almost invariably has large assets behind it to help guarantee that the institution's representative will perform in the way desired. In most instances, too, a bank or trust company is in a better position to handle investments than a private individual either acting as an executor or handling a trust.

Usually, you cannot designate a bank or trust company as executor, unless that institution is authorized to do business in the state where you live. A number of states do permit this designation of a bank or trust company, however, if a co-executor is also nominated from the state where you live.

Any of these options in the selection of an executor may be completely satisfactory, depending on your individual situation. At times in the past there has been some antagonism in individual instances, since lawyers sometimes feel that trust companies or trust officers of a bank may be cutting into the lawyer's work.

CO-EXECUTORS

Sometimes two executors or executrixes are appointed by a testator who does not want to offend a close relative. One of these fiduciaries may be appointed because that individual has an excellent background in finance, while the other person selected may be someone close to the family and to the testator's wishes.

Frequently the appointment of such co-executors or co-executrixes may result in an excellent balance of personal and financial aspects of the fiduciary responsibility. At other times, the joint appointment may not operate so smoothly. Before appointing more than one such fiduciary, the testator should con-

sider the personal characteristics and abilities of those to whom
duties are entrusted.

On occasion, testators may go so far as to appoint three or
more co-executors, specifying that a majority opinion among the
three shall control. This may allow one executor to handle matters that have been already approved while the others are out of
town. But it may also create problems in settling the estate,
needlessly complicating some activities.

LIMITS ON THE EXECUTOR'S DUTIES

Unless an executor or executrix is given some additional
powers in the will, duties and powers are limited and temporary
in character. That is why it may be advantageous to specify in
your will that the executor or executrix is empowered to continue
your business. Unless the executor has this power, he or she is
only authorized to liquidate the business for the benefit of your
heirs. If the executor continues your business, lacking this power
from your will, the executor will be liable for damages if losses
are sustained in the continued operation. This liability for loss
exists, even though the executor made the decisions that any
reasonable, prudent businessperson would have made in the operation of the business.

If, however, your will authorizes the executor to carry on the
business, then the executor will be able to make any reasonable
decision and take normal risks incident to the business, without
being subject to a lawsuit. Of course, the executor can be sued if
he or she is guilty of extreme negligence or commits fraud, but
you do not want to "tie the executor's hands when your estate
most needs help."

GUARDIANS:
FOR MINOR CHILDREN
AND FOR PROPERTY

If you should leave minor children, they may need assistance from someone who can furnish financial guidance, as well as someone who will step into the shoes of missing parents. A probate court can designate a guardian, if you have not done so, but the court's selection may be a cold, technical choice that is not what you would have intended. Actually, there are two types of guardianships: a personal guardianship and a property guardianship. You can designate someone in your will to handle both of these functions, or you can name separate guardians. The personal guardian named, of course, is almost always a member of the family or a close personal friend—someone who can give needed guidance of a very personal sort. The property guardian should preferably be someone with a business or legal background, someone who can handle investments and property.

The responsibilities of the two types of guardianships, of course, call for different types of talent. You may name one person to perform both functions, or you may nominate separate individuals in your will. A bank or trust company may serve as the property guardian. If you leave property in trust for a minor child, the trustee can look after necessary business interests.

CLAIMS ENFORCEABLE
AGAINST THE ESTATE

One of the basic responsibilities of an executor is to pay the deceased's valid debts. Caution should be exercised in payments of sums claimed to be due, however, if you serve as an executor for a relative or a friend. Claims are deductible for estate tax purposes only if both of two conditions are met:

1. The claims must be enforceable against the estate, that is, if they could be recovered by lawsuit and are not merely gratuitous.

2. The claims must be allowable under the state law where the estate is being settled.

In a typical situation of this kind, one child of the decedent may submit a bill to the estate, claiming to have rendered more help or care than other relatives prior to the decedent's death. In most states this claim would not be enforceable, unless services were shown to be rendered under a contract between the child and deceased.

Realizing that one child may have done more than others in the months or years prior to death, a kind-hearted executor may take the initiative to pay out estate funds to this benefactor. This, of course, is only a moral debt at most, and the executor cannot make payments of the this kind, unless a contract existed.

It is also not uncommon for one relative to claim the repayment of monies loaned to the deceased. Most states have so-called *Deadman's laws* that will not permit the payment of claims of this kind unless there is some writing or documentary evidence of the debt. Otherwise, it is likely that frauds could be easily perpetrated against the deceased's estate.

TAX HANDLING OF DECEDENT'S LAST ILLNESS

One of the tax decisions that may be made by an executor is in claiming the medical expenses of the decedent's last illness as a tax deduction of the estate. This deduction may be claimed against either the federal estate tax or the decedent's federal income tax. Interest paid on loans obtained by the executor to pay estate taxes or other administrative costs may also be deductible. The differences vary from case to case, and turn on a number of technical considerations. The possibilities should be considered by the executor, perhaps with the aid of a tax consultant.

PAYING INCOME TAX ON INTEREST ON INHERITANCE NOT YET RECEIVED

Frequently, there is lag between the final settlement of an estate and the notice that money due an heir has been placed in a bank account to earn interest. Once the heir has been designated and the money set aside in an account, the interest is subject to tax payment by the heir. This interest must be included in the heir's income tax return, even though the inheritance has not yet been received. Additional aspects of estate taxation problems are discussed in detail in chapters on federal estate taxation, federal gift taxation, and the use of a trust to avoid taxes.

II

Taxation And Property Accumulation: Saving on Gift And Estate Taxes

10

Taxation— The Hindrance to Estate Building

Taxes are the charges that we pay for a government and a civilized society.[1] Because of these taxes, the distributable funds in an estate are almost always less than an individual held during his or her lifetime.

In only a few generations, most of our federal taxes have changed from simple, revenue-raising devices into governmental tools that control the economic and social conditions of the entire country. In effect, taxes have become an economic leveler, making it difficult for one generation to pass along accumulated savings to children, to grandchildren, or to anyone else.

[1]U.S. Supreme Court Justice Oliver Wendell Holmes, Jr., in Compania de Tabacos v. Collector, 275 U. S. 87, 100 (1904).

While most of us have no intention of evading taxes, there is simply no point in paying more than we are obligated to pay under the law. As the famous federal judge Learned Hand wrote in a 1947 court decision:

> Over and over again courts have said there is nothing sinister in arranging one's affairs as to keep taxes as low as possible. Everybody does so, rich or poor; and all do right, for nobody owes any public duty to pay more than the law demands; taxes are enforced exactions, not voluntary contributions. To demand more in the name of morals is mere cant.

Obviously then a basic aspect of estate planning is to reduce taxes to the lowest possible figure that is legal. But this plan should be considered in the light of overall objectives—in some instances the reduction of taxes to a bare minimum may increase other estate costs to a greater extent.

TYPES OF TAXES INVOLVING ESTATES

In estate preservation and distribution we are usually concerned with three potential federal taxes:

1. estate taxes,

2. gift taxes, and

3. capital gains taxes that may come due when persons inheriting property (legatees) sell off those assets that have been inherited.

In addition, in the settlement of an estate, all states except Nevada impose either a state inheritance tax or a state estate tax, with some states utilizing both an inheritance and an estate tax. Many of the states have also passed gift tax laws, beginning with Oregon in 1933.

CREDIT FOR PAYMENT OF STATE DEATH TAXES

Federal tax laws do permit state death tax payments to be credited against Federal estate taxes. The amounts of these credits are set out in Appendix 7.

FEDERAL INCOME TAXES

In addition, federal and state income taxes must be paid on the earned income, including wages or salary received or earned by the deceased during that part of the year while the deceased was alive. Of all these taxes, the federal estate tax is usually the most powerful drain on estate assets. When all these taxes are lumped together with charges for probate, it is not surprising that an estate planner should consider all legal methods to minimize them.

DIFFERENCES BETWEEN FEDERAL AND STATE DEATH TAXES

To understand federal and state death taxes, it is first necessary to note the difference between an estate tax and an inheritance tax. An *estate tax* is a charge against the estate of the deceased. It is a levy against the total estate. The estate tax is not concerned with how much a particular beneficiary receives, or the beneficiary's relationship to the deceased. It is also sometimes described as a levy on the right to pass along the deceased's property to those designated to receive it. In short, it is a tax on the transfer of property.

On the other hand, an *inheritance tax* is not a tax against the estate as a whole but only against the part of the property to be received by each beneficiary. In the pattern followed in many of the states, inheritance taxes are set up by classes of beneficiaries—that is, set up by degrees of kinship to the deceased. For example, in one state the law may specify that a wife, son, or daughter may be placed in one class and assessed at a lower rate than a beneficiary who is a second cousin.

Most of us, of course, want eventually to pass on our property to individuals close to us. In the majority of instances, these individuals are our children or grandchildren. It is sometimes poor judgment to pass on our assets in advance, if there is a likelihood that we may yet need the income for living expenses or that our estate may need the money to pay taxes. If we are too quick to give away our resources, we may not have the funds to pay for a prolonged illness or for those unforeseen costs that may fall on anyone. And of course, funds should be protected to provide for a continuing good life.

But once a decision has been made to pass on an accumulation to family members, it may be financially advantageous to begin such transfers immediately, and to continue transfers over a number of years. By beginning these transfers at an early date, it is usually possible to pass on a considerably larger total than if we wait to make the transfer by will. This situation exists because of exceptions in the federal gift tax laws, as we will observe. Of course, some individuals may be completely opposed to the thought of turning over even modest amounts of money to their offspring, or to relatives in another generation. But this turnover will take place eventually, unless relatives are disinherited by will.

Undoubtedly, there are times when estate planning in an explosive family situation is of questionable benefit. But if the giver is legally able to supervise or assist the recipient's financial planning, it may be preferable to give an immature heir a training period during the giver's lifetime. As the giver, you will almost always save money for your family by planning gifts, if you intend to pass on your money anyway.

11

Property Ownership
And Its Relation
To Estate Planning

A number of estate tax problems hinge on the way in which property is owned. Altogether different consequences may result if the property you own is in a common law state as opposed to a community property state. In other situations, there may be a difference, depending on whether the property is owned individually or jointly. Therefore, we should examine some basic ideas of property ownership, and how this ownership may affect federal estate taxes, gift taxes, and income taxes.

For purposes of discussion, all states may be classified as having either *common law* systems of property ownership, or *community* property ownership. The bulk of the states (42) operate their legal systems under common law ideas. Puerto Rico and eight states have community property laws:

Arizona	Nevada
California	New Mexico
Idaho	Texas
Louisiana	Washington

PROPERTY OWNERSHIP IN COMMON LAW STATES

In common law states, all property acquired from the husband's earnings during marriage is his property. The same is true for the earnings of the wife. But if the marriage is one in which the wife is not employed, the husband owns everything. Consequently, the husband usually has full legal power to dispose of this property and keep the proceeds, whether the wife agrees or not, but this is true with some exceptions, as we will see.

THE RIGHT OF DOWER

Only if she inherits property or purchases it with her earnings does the wife in a common law state have any ready-made protection against the possibility that a husband may sell the property and disinherit her.

This basic concept of property ownership in common law states goes back hundreds of years to feudal England. When the Normans conquered England in 1066, the Norman king was regarded as owner of all the land. To control the country, the king turned over specific areas to individual lords. But these lords did not own that territory, according to present-day ideas of property ownership; they simply "held" it for the king. The lords then parceled out the land in small tracts to farmers who occupied it and worked it. Under this feudal system, individual farmers gave allegiance to their lord and turned over a specified percentage of their crops and produce to him. Under this pledge of allegiance, the individual farmer held his plot under a promise to defend the lord and serve in the lord's army in time of a military threat. If needed, the king combined the armies of all the lords into a national army. So long as the individual land holder met his obligations to his lord, the individual continued to hold and use the land, passing the land on to his sons or other heirs. After hundreds of years the system was modified, so that individual farmers became outright owners of the land. And in their turn, the lords themselves were awarded ownership of large landed estates.

In this scheme, there never was a place for women to serve in the lord's army or to get possession and use of the land. Even after land came to be privately owned in England, women were not permitted to acquire it until comparatively modern times.

As social conditions changed, individuals gained the right to make wills, disposing of the property they owned. Some husbands found it inconvenient to provide for their widows. The financial plight of a surviving wife would have been precarious, except for the right of dower. Under the old English legal principle of *dower,* which developed about this time, a surviving widow was automatically entitled to a life estate in one-third of any parcel of land that her husband had owned at any time during marriage. This *right to a life estate* meant that the widow had the right to occupy one-third of the real estate that had been owned by her husband—to occupy it, to farm it, to obtain rent money from it, or to use it in any way that did not destroy its substance. Of course, the widow's life estate ended when she died.

A number of states in the United States still permit this right of dower. In other common law states, such as Colorado, Connecticut, and New York, the dower right has been abolished or modified by statute. In some states in the midwest, the wife's dower right varies from a life estate in one-third of the husband's lands to a life estate in one-half or in all of the husband's lands.

But the dower right applies to real property only, and not to personal property such as stocks, bonds, corporate interests, or other forms of wealth that her husband may have owned. Dower worked reasonably well against disinheritance in early-day England, where almost all wealth was measured in ownership of lands and the right to land or property rentals. While real estate is, of course, still a highly desirable form of wealth, the financial thrust of society changed long ago. The bulk of wealth today is often held in stocks and bonds, in corporate ownership, in bank accounts, and in other types of assets. Today, a surviving wife may be left almost penniless in a common law state if she should be disinherited and if the right of dower is her only protection.

When a buyer purchases property in a common law state, lawyers for the buyer almost always insist that the wife sign off her dower right on the transfer papers, even though the husband is the sole owner. This, of course prevents the wife from coming back and claiming an interest in the property when she is widowed. In some situations of this kind, the husband actually forced the wife to sign off her dower right.

In those states where the right to dower still exists, the surviving wife ordinarily has the choice between any money and property that may have been left to her in her husband's will or by the dower right, whichever is to her advantage. But the fact remains that in a state that still permits dower the husband may be able to hurt his wife financially if he sold his real estate and put the proceeds into some other form of wealth, thereafter disinheriting the wife in his will.

To help correct this weakness, some states have a statute specifying that any transfer of real estate by a husband within two years of his death is a fraud on the wife, and dower right in such property can still be claimed against the buyer.

In addition, all but seven of the common law states have passed laws giving the surviving spouse a set percentage of the deceased husband's assets, and this percentage automatically passes to the wife by operation of law, regardless of attempts to disinherit. The fraction of the husband's assets granted to the wife by these statutes is usually either one-third or one-half of the husband's property. From state to state, these laws vary in detail, however.

In some states a surviving husband has the *right of curtesy,* that is generally comparable to the wife's right of dower. This right does not usually correspond entirely with the right of dower, since curtesy does not come into being unless the couple had offspring.

Some private retirement plans also extend some financial protection to a disinherited wife in a common law state, since certain rights may be vested, whether or not the husband attempts to change the beneficiary.

In a common law state, the full value of the husband's property is taxed as belonging to his estate, under provisions of the federal estate tax. This full taxation is provided for by law, even though the wife claims a dower interest or takes a statutory share in lieu of the property given to her by will.

Community Property Ownership

The basic idea underlying the community property system is that while the husband's earnings may be the immediate source of the couple's income and acquisitions, the labor, effort, and industry of both spouses contribute to the acquisition of property during marriage. In a community property state, half the property acquired during marriage is, in effect, owned by each spouse. This is true, even though only one of the marriage partners may work or have income. The theory is that both partners contribute to the financial success of the marriage, regardless of whether both are paid, engage in business, or earn money.

The only holdings not considered community property in these states consist of property the husband or wife already owned separately before marriage or inherited individually after marriage. All other property acquired after marriage is community property.

In community property states (other than New Mexico) each of the marriage partners is the owner of an undivided one-half interest in the common property. Each spouse also has the power to dispose of this one-half of the community property by will, as well as the right to dispose of separate property.

It really does not matter which spouse's name appears on the deed in most instances in a community property state. It is not separate property if acquired during the marriage.

All community property states do have some individual peculiarities in their interpretation of community property. Texas, for example, does not permit community funds to be used to create a joint tenancy with a right of survivorship between the spouses. And in other community property states there are legal differences on a number of other points. Generalization concerning community property states is both difficult and dangerous.

Under state inheritance treatment, a number of community property states give some preferred treatment to the community property. California and Idaho, for example, do not tax community property at all if it is left to the other spouse.

A study of tax laws concerned with community property emphasizes the fact that specific records of property purchases, payments, improvements, and sales should be kept, along with receipts. Given the fact that marriage partners own separate property, own some community property, and commingle their funds, problems may arise. After the passage of time, it may be almost impossible to determine which assets are separately owned, which are community property, and which are a combination of both.

JOINT OWNERSHIP

Regardless of whether property is located in a common law state or a community property state, the property may be owned in the name of one spouse only (that is, *individually owned*), or it may be owned by a husband and wife together (*jointly owned*). There are a number of reasons for joint ownership. Married couples frequently feel that such ownership expresses the idea of marriage as a partnership. It often promotes a sense of unity and family harmony. From a practical standpoint, there is no waiting to go through legal processes in the event of death of one of the spouses. The surviving party to the marriage automatically owns the entire property upon the death of the other, under the forms of joint ownership that we will examine in this chapter.

TYPES OF JOINT OWNERSHIP

The term "joint ownership" is often loosely used to include many shades of meaning to the general public. Basically, any joint ownership falls into one of three kinds, with the owners having some different rights in each category. It is important to distinguish between these kinds of joint ownership, because of differing implications under estate and inheritance tax laws. These three classes of joint ownership are:

1. Joint tenancy with the right of survivorship, frequently shortened to "joint tenancy" with the "right of survivorship" understood, in legal meaning,

2. tenancy in the entirety, and

3. tenancy in common.

JOINT TENANCY WITH THE RIGHT OF SURVIVORSHIP— OR SIMPLY, JOINT TENANCY

The most common form of joint ownership is legally called *joint tenancy*. In common usage, it may be termed *joint tenancy with the right of survivorship*. The last five words of this phrase are superfluous. The legal meaning is exactly the same, since "joint tenancy" has implied in it the "right of survivorship."

In most states there is no requirement that the joint tenants must be man and wife. For example, three people—a husband, a wife, and a son—could all purchase property as joint tenants. This might be done with the expectation that the entire property would someday pass to the surviving spouse and son, and finally to the son alone.

There are some legal advantages for a married couple that purchases as joint tenants. For example, creditors of an individual joint tenant of this kind cannot reach that particular piece of property after the debtor's death, even though creditors might thereafter go to the trouble to obtain a judgment against that debtor. To subject this jointly owned property to their claims, creditors would be required to first bring a legal action to sever the joint tenancy, and this must be done during the debtor's lifetime. Finally, we have also previously noted that joint ownership with the right of survivorship takes the property out of probate. In many instances, the use of joint ownership may be good estate planning, since the costs and delays of probate are avoided.

TENANCY IN THE ENTIRETY AS ANOTHER FORM OF JOINT OWNERSHIP

In some states there is a slightly different kind of joint ownership, called *tenancy in the entirety*. In most states where this form of joint ownership is used, it is limited to joint ownership by a husband and wife only. In addition this kind of ownership of property is also limited to real property (real estate), and it does not apply to personal property. In *tenancy in the entirety*, neither spouse alone has a disposable interest in the property. In other words, both spouses must join together in signing to sell or dispose of the property. Whether the joint ownership is called joint tenancy with right of survivorship or tenancy by the entirety, the tenants (owners) continue to own the property until one is cut out of ownership automatically by death. At that time, the survivor owns 100 percent.

TENANCY IN COMMON AS A FORM OF JOINT OWNERSHIP

Neither of these kinds of joint ownership should be confused with the third kind of joint ownership, called "tenancy in common." Ownership under *tenancy in common* consists of an undivided or unsegregated interest in the whole. On the death of one owner, his or her heirs still own a fractional part of the whole property. No property rights or interests are extinguished by death of one of the joint owners. If the individual owner wants to obtain his or her part of the property, it may be done through a voluntary agreement among the owners for a partition or division into individual segments, or there must be a court-ordered partition. Lawyers say that this partition does not create a new interest or title, but merely severs the prior unity of enjoyment and possession.

JOINT TENANCY OR TENANCY BY THE ENTIRETY IN A SECOND MARRIAGE

Joint tenancy or tenancy by the entirety may not be suitable for parties in a second marriage. It has been pointed out that the entire ownership passes to the survivor when property is owned jointly, either in joint tenancy or in tenancy by the entirety. Both of these arrangements have the advantage of avoiding probate. Be very hesitant to go into a joint tenancy or tenancy in the entirety arrangement, unless husband and wife are both in a first marriage. The husband, for example, may intend to leave all his property to his wife, with the property eventually going to his children upon the wife's death. But if the wife has children of her own by a prior marriage, then her children would inherit the entire property upon her death, unless some different legal arrangement had been made.

Consequently, it may not be advisable for one of the partners of a second marriage to purchase property jointly with his or her spouse, if the first party intends for his or her offspring to eventually get the property.

DOUBLE TAXATION CAN RESULT FROM JOINT OWNERSHIP

On the disadvantageous side of the estate planning picture, there may be two compelling arguments against a man and wife owning property as joint tenants or as tenants in the entirety:

1. In calculating the federal estate tax, Internal Revenue authorities treat the entire piece of jointly owned property as a taxable asset owned by the first of the joint owners to die. From our joint ownership concepts, we know that the survivor takes all or has a fee simple interest in the entire property. Yet the federal tax laws treat the entire property as owned by the deceased, rather than by the survivor. This would appear to be something of an injustice, but federal tax law decisions on this point are well settled. However, federal tax authorities do permit the survivor to prove that the deceased paid for less than 100 percent of the property. If the survivor has records to show that a fractional part of

the property payments were made by the survivor, then up to one-half of the value of the property may be deducted. But in most cases, married couples have so intermixed their funds that it is difficult to prove which spouse actually made payments on joint property. As head of the household, the husband usually makes the payments on jointly owned property such as a home, and it is almost impossible to satisfy federal tax officials of the wife's contributions.

If the executor or administrator of an estate is someone other than a surviving spouse, that person will be even less likely than a family member to have all the needed financial records of the family.

2. When property is owned jointly by a man and wife, there may be unnecessary taxation against the couple's total estates that are eventually passed on to their children or other heirs. In most instances of joint ownership, the property has already been taxed 100 percent in the estate of the first spouse to die. Then it is taxed again at a 100 percent rate in the estate of the second spouse. As a result, the couples' children or other heirs will eventually take less than if the property had been taxed half in the estate of the first to die, and half in the estate of the second.

Under the provisions of the *Tax Reform Act of 1976,* a husband and wife may elect to regard jointly owned property under another alternative. This option does not apply to joint ownership as tenants in common. Under this option, the couple may treat a part of the purchase price as a gift made by the principal contributor to the other spouse. If the gift here is of sufficient value, then both will be regarded as contributing on a fifty-fifty basis. Upon the death of either spouse, then only one-half of the value of the jointly owned property will be included in the taxable gross estate of the decedent. Under some circumstances, a gift of this kind from one spouse to another may be subject to the federal gift tax, as will be noted in our chapter on federal gift taxes.

From an estate planning standpoint, sometimes it may be advantageous for a couple to switch from joint ownership of property to ownership of only one-half by each spouse. But a decision of this kind may have an adverse effect on gift taxes, income taxes, or estate tax liability, and should not be considered without the advice of a tax lawyer.

JOINT OWNERSHIP VS. TRANSFER BY WILL

In most instances, it is advantageous for people who own property to prepare a will for the transfer of property. On an individual case basis, however, this may not always be desirable.

Recently an elderly husband and wife went to a lawyer after reading a magazine article about estate planning, which stressed the need to draft a will. Questioning by the lawyer revealed that the husband and wife had accumulated a modest estate, consisting of furniture and household goods, a small home worth under $40,000, and personal savings accounts that totaled about $8,000. The husband and wife were each 65, with two children, a married son aged 32 and a married daughter aged 29. The husband posed the question about whether he and his wife really needed a will, since their home and bank accounts were owned as joint tenants with the right of survivorship.

Without making a positive recommendation, for or against a will, the lawyer pointed out some of the legal possibilities in this situation. One option for the parents would be to have a new deed drafted for the home, adding the name of their son and possibly the name of their daughter as joint tenants with right of survivorship. This would have the advantage of passing the home without probate and the payment of attendant probate fees, as well as the cost of drafting a will. But this could create some resulting problems. If either parent should die, the surviving spouse might want to remarry and give the new wife or husband an ownership interest in the home. If the son's name had been added to the deed, the son could refuse to grant permission for the new spouse to be given part ownership.

In addition, if the parents should want to sell their home and move elsewhere, this move could be blocked by any child whose name had been added to the deed. Obviously then, the addition of names of additional joint tenants could restrict the parents in disposing of their home. If the name of one or both of the children was added to the deed, and he or she subsequently went into bankruptcy or had financial difficulties, the child's problems could work a serious financial hardship on the otherwise independent parents. Creditors of the child could force a legal suit for partition of the home, requiring it to be sold and the child's portion used to satisfy a judgment.

Another possibility would be that the child might be injured in an automobile accident, suffering something serious such as brain damage. In that instance, it would be necessary for a guardian to be appointed for the child, to handle affairs. It is highly unlikely that a judge supervising guardianship matters would allow the guardian to sign off papers for the house unless actual compensation was received by the child's estate.

Another possibility, though remote, is that all three, both parents and the son could be killed in a common disaster, such as an automobile wreck, with the son dying last. This would possibly deprive the daughter of her right to half of the property, if only the son's name had been added to those of the parents on the newly drafted deed. As another consideration here, some states allow property tax exemptions or reductions to senior citizens. Under the laws of some states, this tax-reduction right would be lost through the act of conveying a joint ownership interest to one or more of the couple's children.

There are some other tax considerations that could figure in the outcome. If a gift tax return was not filed by the parents, reflecting a gift to one or both of the children, then this failure could complicate the transaction. In addition in an eventual sale of the parent's home by the son and daughter, the latter two heirs could receive an income tax benefit through acquisition of the property by a will, rather than as joint tenants.

From all of these possibilities, it appears that it might be a questionable choice to add the son's and/or daughter's name to the deed on the parent's home. This is, of course, a personal choice. The problem might be somewhat simplified if there was only one parent and one child and if the parent had no intention of ever remarrying. But in most instances of this kind, the use of a will executed by each parent would be preferable.

All of these considerations have been directed toward the ultimate estate problem—that of passing the property on to the couple's two children. The immediate problem for the older couple here is to pass the property from one spouse to the other. That, of course, has been solved for the present by owning the home and the bank accounts in joint tenancy. It may be preferable to have no additional action taken until after the death of one spouse. Then consider having a new deed prepared, adding the name of either the couple's son or names of both children, as joint tenants with the right of survivorship.

POWER OF ATTORNEY

At some point in your life, it may be either desirable or necessary to have someone handle your affairs, at least on a temporary basis. A "power of attorney authorization" is frequently the best solution to such a problem.

Legally, a *power of attorney* is a kind of agency. It is a written authorization you give to an individual or an institution such as a bank, to conduct business in your behalf. It is not a trust. The power of attorney relationship does not require the supervision of a court, nor does it require a court accounting of transactions. The person to whom such power is granted need not be a lawyer, although this person is called an *attorney-in-fact*. This term is not to be confused with an "attorney-at-law," who of course is a lawyer.

The power of attorney granted to another may be a general one, to handle all your business, or a specific one for only one purpose or for limited special purposes. The authority may also be set up to cover a set length of time, or it may be allowed to run indefinitely.

Any act undertaken by the person who holds your power of attorney has the same legal effect as if you had done it yourself— unless the power of attorney was a limited one and the holder of the power clearly exceeded the authority that had been given by you. For example, if your job takes you to Europe and you give your brother power of attorney to sell your home, your brother's signature on the deed, as holder of your power of attorney, is binding on you.

There are some limits beyond which an individual holding your power of attorney can go, but these restrictions are few. For example, the holder of the power cannot draw up a deed making a gift of your property; you must receive some compensation, but it need not necessarily be the full amount of compensation that you would have demanded from a purchaser. The holder cannot deed your property to himself or herself, or to a principal working with the holder, and there are restrictions on mortgaging or deeding a homestead. But the holder of a power of attorney has great power. An example of a general power of attorney form is located in Appendix 8. Because of the serious responsibility inherent in the use of this form, all states require a power of attorney form to be signed in the presence of a notary public or some other authority. It should then be placed on file with the county recorder or state recording official, along with the necessary recording fee. Thereafter, the general public is on notice of the authority of the person holding the power.

A power of attorney is not designed to take the place of a will, since the holder of the authority has no legal power after the death of the individual granting the power. In most states, the power of attorney also becomes invalid if the maker becomes mentally incompetent. An individual holding a power of attorney simply has authority to act, and is not required to assume responsibility of a guardianship or a conservatorship.

PRACTICAL USES FOR A POWER OF ATTORNEY AUTHORIZATION

There are times when the use of a power of attorney authorization may be very helpful:

1. An aged person who is in good condition may give the authorization to someone else, merely to avoid the long hours of business.

2. A mining engineer going into the interior of the Peruvian jungle may also make use of this tool.

3. A semi-retired businessman who wants to take a luxury cruise around the world may also have need of a power of attorney authorization given to a business associate.

4. If an individual is ill, close family members may want to help in obtaining papers from a safe deposit box, in handling banking transactions or other business concerns. Usually, even the closest of relatives cannot do these things unless provided with a signed power of attorney form. This is also a legal tool that may be used to protect your estate if you have been subjected to a heart attack or a stroke, with future physical impairment as a possibility.

Some individuals, who are on a very close personal basis with their lawyer or banker, leave a signed power of attorney form granting authority to a close relative or friend. This form is to be held by the lawyer or banker indefinitely, and is to be delivered to the person given authority only in the event the lawyer or banker believes a definite need has developed. In a state where mental incompetency invalidates a power of attorney, an individual may want to consider setting up a revocable living trust while there is as yet no question as to mental competency.

Considerable caution should go along with the use of a power of attorney. There is always a risk, however remote, that a person holding a power of this kind may cause financial ruin to the individual who has granted the authority.

12

The Federal
Estate Tax

The federal estate tax was first imposed at the time of the Spanish-American War. It was repealed after a short trial period in 1902 but revived in 1916. In early-day versions, the tax was structured so that it affected few except the very well-to-do. As revisions were made, the tax began to reach some families of only a little more than moderate means. Sweeping changes were made in the *Federal Tax Reform Act of 1976.* This revised law was phased in over a five-year period and is to be completely set in 1981. At the time of the law's passage in 1976, it was apparently intended to exempt estates of moderate size. But with inflation and the current upswing in values, the tax is beginning to be felt in an increasing number of estates.

Under current conditions, the estate of a married couple may be whittled away, as the property passes to the surviving spouse and eventually to the children or other heirs. Federal estate taxes may be imposed on each of these transfers. Getting money through this tax screen to the heirs is frequently the most troublesome aspect of estate planning.

In actual operation, the federal estate tax is often quite complicated because it involves exacting refinements and delicate distinctions. Prior to the passage of the *Tax Reform Act of 1976,* there were two separate tax rate structures that applied to most estates. One of these was the federal gift tax, which applied to gifts made during the lifetime of the person owning the estate. The other tax schedule was the federal estate tax, which was applied to property transferred at the time of death by will or by devise and descent.

The *Tax Reform Act of 1976* changed the two tax rate system, leaving us with a single unified tax schedule. Separate gift tax and estate tax exemptions that had existed previously were eliminated. Their places were taken by a unified credit for both gifts made during your lifetime and for transfers at the time of death.

CHANGES IN CALCULATING ESTATE TAX LIABILITY

Prior to January 1, 1977, under the old Federal estate tax law, there was a basic exemption of $60,000. This was an exemption on the value of the estate, not on the amount of tax imposed or to be collected. In other words, under the old law no tax need be figured, and there was no tax due, if the estate did not exceed $60,000 in worth. Taxes were assessed on the value of the estate that exceeded $60,000, after debts and funeral expenses.

Today, federal estate tax liability is not figured that way. The tax is figured on the actual worth of the estate, beginning at zero. There is no longer any deduction on the value of the estate. Then after the tax is figured, an exemption is allowed, once the tax due has been calculated. This single unified tax is calculated on the combined values of both lifetime transfers, that is, gifts that are not otherwise exempt and properties and money left at the time of death. In other words, this tax is cumulative, including the tax assessed on the basis of the combined values.

This cumulative gift and estate tax does not include matters such as adjustment for gift tax paid by spouse, and so on, and is figured in Table 12-1.

TABLE 12-1. Gift tax calculations.

Total Value of Gifts + Value of Estate Left at Death	The Tentative Tax Is:
Not over $10,000	18 percent of such amount.
Over $10,000 but not over $20,000	$1,800, plus 20 percent of the excess of such amount over $10,000.
over $20,000 but not over $40,000	$3,800, plus 22 percent of the excess of such amount over $20,000.
Over $40,000 but not over $60,000	$8,200 plus 24 percent of the excess of such amount over $40,000.
Over $60,000 but not over $80,000	$13,000, plus 25 percent of the excess of such amount over $60,000.
Over $80,000 but not over $100,000	$18,200, plus 28 percent of the excess of such amount over $80,000.
Over $100,000 but not over $150,000	$23,800, plus 30 percent of the excess of such amount over $100,000.

TABLE 12-1. continued

Total Value of Gifts + Value of Estate Left at Death	*The Tentative Tax Is:*
Over $150,000 but not over $250,000	$38,800, plus 32 percent of the excess of such amount over $150,000.
Over $250,000 but not over $500,000	$70,800, plus 34 percent of the excess of such amount over $250,000.
Over $500,000 but not over $750,000	$155,800, plus 37 percent of the excess of such amount over $500,000.
Over $750,000 but not over $1,000,000	$248,300, plus 39 percent of the excess of such amount over $750,000.
Over $1,000,000 but not over $1,250,000	$345,800, plus 41 percent of the excess of such amount over $1,000,000.
Over $1,250,000 but not over $1,500,000	$448,300, plus 43 percent of the excess of such amount over $1,250,000.
Over $1,500,000 but not over $2,000,000	$555,800, plus 45 percent of the excess of such amount over $1,500,000.
Over $2,000,000 but not over $2,500,000	$780,800, plus 49 percent of the excess of such amount over $2,000,000.
Over $2,500,000 but not over $3,000,000	$1,025,800, plus 53 percent of the excess of such amount over $2,500,000.

TABLE 12-1. continued

Total Value of Gifts + Value of Estate Left at Death	The Tentative Tax Is:
Over $3,00,000 but not over $3,500,000	$1,290,800, plus 57 percent of the excess of such amount over $3,000,000.
Over $3,500,000 but not over $4,000,000	$1,575,800, plus 61 percent of the excess of such amount over $3,500,000.
Over $4,000,000 but not over $4,500,000	$1,880,800, plus 65 percent of the excess of such amount over $4,000,000.
Over $4,500,000 but not over $5,000,000	$2,205,800, plus 69 percent of the excess of such amount over $4,500,000.
Over $5,000,000	$2,550,800, plus 70 percent of the excess of such amount over $5,000,000.

THE BASE (GROSS ESTATE) ON WHICH FEDERAL ESTATE TAX IS CALCULATED

Your federal estate tax is imposed on all your property and assets at the time of death, minus your debts, funeral expenses, and other legal obligations. Your assets and property that are subject to tax include:

1. all property which you own outright at the time of your

death. This includes your home or other real estate, stocks, bonds, cash in banks, and personal property such as automobiles, jewelry, art, furniture, and so on;

2. any property which passes to your spouse under the state laws of intestacy, or property that goes to a spouse under state laws permitting an election for a percentage of your property, in lieu of taking under the provisions of your will;

3. any unused part of a pension or annuity that is payable;

4. the proceeds from life insurance on your life, unless the policies were actually owned by someone else. You continue to own them so long as you pay premiums, had the right to change beneficiary, and had the right to assign the policy, and so on—as long as you retained the *indicia of ownership;*

5. any gifts to which you retained a life interest—that is, property that you gave to someone else during your lifetime, in which you retained a legal life interest or the right to income for life. Also, property to which you retained the right to select who will succeed to the life interest you gave away during your lifetime;

6. property you owned jointly prior to January 1, 1977 with the right of survivorship to you or another. Your estate will not be charged with that part of the jointly owned property that was paid for by the survivor with his or her own funds. The U.S. Internal Revenue Service places the burden on the survivor to trace through the monies paid by that survivor. Otherwise, the whole value of the jointly owned property will be included in your estate for tax purposes. If the joint tenancy with right of survivorship was acquired after January 1, 1977, however, then only one-half of the value will be charged to your estate;

7. business interests that have financial worth, such as a valuable contract, or a business partnership interest, the right to a lawsuit against someone, or other interests that have value;

8. gifts taking effect at death, such as giving away an antique car during your lifetime, with the agreement that you retained the use of it and ownership was to pass on your death;

9. the value of property controlled under a power of appointment—that is, an authority or power conferred by will or by deed, giving you the right to select the individual or individuals who are to receive a specific estate or the income from a specific fund or estate, after the termination of an existing right or interest, and

10. gifts made after January 1, 1977. There are, however, exceptions to this, as some gifts are exempt from taxes. (See the exemptions enumerated under the gift tax section in Chapter 13.)

After all of these items are added up, you are then allowed to deduct:

1. expenses of estate administration (which includes executor's or executrix's expenses),

2. funeral and burial expenses,

3. all legitimate claims against the estate,

4. all mortgages against property that has been listed at its value with mortgages or loans unpaid,

5. charitable bequests by will,

6. losses by casualty or theft for which the estate has not been compensated,

7. the marital deduction—a special deduction that may be claimed by married couples under specific circumstances. (See the material in the chapter entitled Marital Deductions.)

The federal estate tax is then computed, based on the value

of property that still remains after deductions have been made. This is your gross estate.

Sometimes the estate of a deceased person will include assets that were previously taxed in the estate of another individual who had died previously. When such assets were included in the prior taxable estate within ten years before the death of the second individual, the federal law permits a credit against the federal estate tax. The amount of credit varies from 100 percent when no more than two years separated the two deaths. This credit reduces to 20 percent if the interval between the two deaths was from nine to ten years. See Appendix 7 for the reduced credits allowed, depending on the intervals between the two deaths.

THE ORPHAN'S DEDUCTION

The *Tax Reform Act of 1976* also provides for an orphan's deduction. Under this provision, there is a deduction of $5,000 multiplied by the number of years an orphan heir is short of the age of 21. This amount is deducted tax free from value of an estate passing to a child of 21 by the child's widowed mother or widower father. This also applies to adopted children, and is an individual exclusion of each orphan child. To calculate the amount for one child, consider the example of a child that was 10 years of age when orphaned. The child lacked 11 years of being 21. The exclusion for that child would then be $5,000 × 11 = $55,000.

THE ESTATE TAX EXEMPTION

Once the amount of tax has been figured, the *Tax Reform Act of 1976* allows you a credit or exemption, that applies against the amount of calculated tax. As compared to the old law, the difference in the way of figuring liability here is that the credit is against the tax that is to be assessed, and not against the value of the estate that may be subject to tax. This credit against the amount of the combined gift and estate tax increases up to 1981, depending on the year in which the taxpayer dies. This combined tax credit is as follows:

Individuals Dying During Year:	Amount of Exemption* Against Tax Assessed	Equivalent Exemption Amount of Estate That Would Pass Tax-Free
1979	$ 38,000.00	$147,333.00
1980	42,500.00	161,563.00
1981 or any year thereafter	47,000.00	175,625.00

*To the extent that all or part of this allowable credit against the tax is used to reduce gift taxes, it is not available to reduce that person's (the donor's) estate taxes.

But this chart, which was set up by the United States Government Committee on Ways and Means on August 2, 1976 to explain estate tax liability, can be very misleading. The government's figures under column three (Equivalent Exemption— Amount of Estate That Would Pass Tax-Free) does not necessarily apply to all estates. The equivalent exemption gradually becomes less as the estate subject to taxation becomes larger. Under the 1976 law, credit is taken against the amount of the tax due, whereas the old exemption previously allowed had been a flat deduction taken off the size of the gross estate, to which estate tax rates were then applied.

The government's chart is accurate for an estate that is no larger than the figures listed in column three. But to show the difference in a larger estate, here is an example:

An individual died in 1979 with a taxable estate of $750,000. The *unified taxes* due, which are the combined gift and estate taxes under the unified rate were $248,300. With an exemption of taxes of $38,000, the estate owed $210,300 in taxes.

However, if the equivalent exemption could be taken, we would figure the rate as: $750,000 less $147,333 (equivalent exemption) = $602,667. From the tax table we would then calculate the tax as $193,786.79. This means that a difference of $16,513 more in taxes would be due, using the $38,000 credit. Thus, in this rather large estate, the $38,000 credit would be equal to an equivalent exemption of considerably less than the figure of $147,333 listed in the chart. Since the unified rates are progressive under the *Tax Reform Act of 1976*, the effect of the unified credit is to exempt less of a larger estate than a smaller one from the federal estate tax given the same credit.

Exclusion for Grandchildren

Transfers from a grandparent to a grandchild may be exempted from federal estate taxation if the transfer to that grandchild does not exceed $250,000. This can be accomplished by a trust set up by the grandparent, providing tax-free income to a child up to $250,000, with the remainder over to the grandchild. How this may be accomplished is discussed in Chapter 17, dealing with tax savings through the use of trusts.

LIFE INSURANCE

A life insurance policy may be a valuable tool in estate planning, since the proceeds are not subject to probate.

Many individuals seem to be under the impression that proceeds from a life insurance policy are not subject to federal estate taxes. As a general proposition, this is simply not true. Federal tax laws specifically include life insurance proceeds in your taxable gross estate, if:

1. your policy is payable to the executor or to the estate, or

2. your policy is payable to a beneficiary other than the executor or to the estate if you as the insured still retained any indicia of ownership or incidents of ownership.[1]

These *incidents of ownership* or *indicia of ownership* are not the usual rights generally associated with the legal meaning of ownership. As used under the federal law, the terms refer to the right of the insured, or his or her estate to the economic benefits of the policy.

In other words, these incidents or indicia of ownership include the right to borrow on the policy against the cash surrender value, the right to change the beneficiary, the right to surrender the policy, the right to convert to some other form of policy, or the right to assign or pledge it. Under the federal law, the proceeds of the policy will be taxed in the estate, although only a single incident of ownership is retained by the policyholder. In the usual situation, then, an individual who takes out a policy has created a taxable asset, because the insured is entitled to incidents of ownership that are part and parcel of the policy.

Court decisions hold that the proceeds will be taxed in the insured's estate, even though the policy is a term or group insurance contract that provides no investment features or cash surrender value. These decisions are based on the fact that the insured has the right to assign the policy or the right to change the beneficiary.

Up until 1954, a provision in the Internal Revenue Code required that the proceeds of a life insurance policy be included in the taxable gross estate of the decedent, if that individual had paid the premiums on the policy. Since 1954, the payment of premiums has not been regarded as an indicia of ownership.

In one case reaching the federal courts on this incidents of

[1]Section 2042 of the Federal Revenue Code of 1954.

ownership restriction, the insured took out a policy and named his family business as beneficiary. The business thereafter made payments of premiums and exercised physical control over the policy as an asset on the company books. When the insured died, proceeds from the policy were held to be taxable in his personal estate, under the federal estate tax. The court's decision was apparently based on the fact that the insured still had the right to change the beneficiary and the right to exercise a conversion privilege.[2]

Because of court decisions of this kind, a number of authorities feel that regular life insurance can be exempted from federal estate taxation only by placing it in trust or by parting with it, either by sale or by gift. If an insured gives up all incidents of ownership of a group term life insurance policy and assigns it to an irrevocable trust, the insured will lose control over the proceeds. Under circumstances of that kind, the premium payments may be treated as a gift by the employer, provided these payments do not exceed the annual exclusion of $3,000 per year. The proceeds from the policy will be exempt from the federal estate tax, but only if it is clear that the insured has surrendered all incidents of ownership, such as the right to convert the group policy to an individual contract.[3]

STATE ESTATE AND INHERITANCE TAXES ON LIFE INSURANCE

A number of states impose inheritance taxes or estate taxes on the proceeds of life insurance policies. Several of these jurisdictions make an exception, however, excusing the proceeds of life

[2]Kearns v. United States, 399 F 2d 226 and United States v. Rhode Island Hospital Trust Company, 355 F 2d 7.
[3]Rev. Rul. 76–490.

insurance from taxation if payable to an individual, such as a spouse. Certain other states allow a specific amount of life insurance to be exempt from state taxes, placing a tax on only proceeds of more than a set amount. This ceiling for exempt proceeds varies from $20,000 to $75,000, depending on the state where the will was probated.

State inheritance tax laws in some states impose a low tax bracket on life insurance proceeds received by close relatives or direct descendants, such as sons, daughters, grandchildren, and so on. Brothers, sisters, cousins, and other relatives may be taxed in a higher tax bracket. It is therefore suggested that if you intend to give money to a relative that would fall into one of these higher tax brackets, consideration should be given to purchasing a life insurance policy that would be exempt from state taxation, rather than leaving the bequest in a will.

13

The Federal Gift Tax

Of the two commonly used methods for transferring money or property to other family members—transfer by gift during the giver's lifetime or transfer by last will and testament—both are subject to federal taxation.

The first federal gift tax law was passed in 1924, but was repealed within two years. Passed a second time in 1932, the gift tax has become a regular part of the federal revenue system. It was intended not only to collect tax money, but also to catch property transfers individuals made during their lifetime to get around the increasing cost of federal estate taxes. The federal gift tax applies to any gratuitous transfer of money or property, or to any interest in property. In short, it covers any situation in which the giver

was not compensated, either partially or completely. For example, if you give money or property such as a city lot to one of your children, it will be subject to federal gift tax. However, there are exclusions that may apply.

Sale to a relative of 1,000 of Union Pacific stock at a price of $25,000 when the market value is $58,000 would constitute a gift of $33,000, and the $33,000 would be taxable.

The test applied by the Internal Revenue Service and the courts is the fair market value at the time the gift was made. If a commodity sells on the open market or at a public exchange, then the market quotations are used to set value. If the item is one that is not commonly bought and sold, then an independent appraisal will be made to determine value. Rates for combined federal gift and estate taxes are set out in Appendix 9.

By making a gift, you remove the value of the gift from your taxable estate. But the giving must represent a legitimate change of ownership and control. A mere designation that the painting over the mantle is going to daughter Bertha is not sufficient to constitute a gift, unless Bertha actually takes the painting and it is thereafter regarded as hers. Otherwise, the property remains as part of the taxable estate, even though a notation may have been made on the back of the painting that "this painting is a gift to Bertha." If you are going to make a gift of real estate, you must use a written instrument, such as a deed, to actually effect the transfer. As a caution here, it is generally advisable to consult a lawyer on any gift having a value of more than $3,000.

A NUMBER OF STATES ALSO IMPOSE GIFT TAXES

Beginning with Oregon in 1933, a number of states adopted gift tax laws. These, of course, are imposed in addition to federal gift tax assessments.

California, Colorado, Delaware, Louisiana, Minnesota, New York, North Carolina, Oklahoma, Oregon, Rhode Island, South Carolina, Tennessee, Vermont, Virginia, Washington, Wisconsin and Puerto Rico all impose gift taxes, with some of these also collecting estate or inheritance taxes.

GIFTS IN TRUST ARE ALSO SUBJECT TO FEDERAL GIFT TAX

The federal gift tax applies to gifts in trust as well as to gifts that are outright donations. In the trust field, a transaction is regarded as a completed gift, subject to taxation, if the trust is an irrevocable one, and if you have not kept a power of appointment, or retained the right to alter or amend the trust agreement.

CHANGES IN GIFT TAX LAWS

Note that there were two separate kinds of federal taxes imposed on estates prior to the passage of the *Tax Reform Act of 1976.* Consequently, two tax rate structures were utilized.

If you intended to eventually pass your property on to children, relatives, or close friends anyway, there was good reason to accomplish part of this objective by making gifts during your lifetime. In the first place, the old gift tax rates, those before 1977, were set up at three-fourths of the amount your estate would pay in death tax or estate tax rates. And up to a point, the gift tax that applied was calculated at the lowest rate in the gift tax bracket. Furthermore, there were annual exclusions and a lifetime exemption that were often helpful in holding down taxes.

As pointed out earlier, under the current law there is a single, unified tax rate that applies to cumulative transfers of money and property, both during the giver's lifetime and at the time of death. There is now a credit that is allowed against this unified tax. Any or all of the credit that is not used up during your lifetime by the giving of gifts subject to tax may be claimed against estate taxes imposed at the time of your death. What this means is that gifts made after January 1, 1977 must be included in your gross estate for calculating the unified tax due, unless these gifts come within specified exemptions. But because of the exemptions allowed under the law, there may still be definite advantages to the use of lifetime gifts by the estate planner. The question is whether you can afford to give away assets during your lifetime. Undoubtedly, the certain way to avoid the federal estate portion of your taxes is to have nothing left in your estate at the time you die. But only a few of us, of course, will be able to make our spending coincide exactly with the time of death.

Nevertheless, the more an estate is cut down in value by tax exempt lifetime giving, the less estate taxes will eventually be paid. Proper timing here is the answer in reducing the tax bill.

THE ANNUAL EXCLUSION UNDER THE FEDERAL GIFT TAX

The current law permits giving property or money in the amount of $3,000 to any one individual per year, without the payment of any federal taxes by the giver. Neither is the recipient required to pay an income tax on this gift. A husband and wife together can make this gift total up to $6,000 per year to any one individual. This $3,000 annual exclusion can be continued year after year, without any limit on the total that can be passed on. If one of the marriage partners makes a gift of this kind, the spouse can also give $3,000 per year to the same beneficiary. As a result, a married couple can give each heir a total of $6,000 per year, without ever becoming subject to any federal gift tax. This giving by a couple is permitted even if only one of the spouses furnishes the entire $6,000 that makes up their joint gift.

To be tax-free, these gifts must be given outright, with no strings attached. If a parent deposits $3,000 per year in a savings account in the name of both parent and child, the transaction would not qualify as a tax-free gift. By opening an account of this kind, the parent simply did not give up control and could take the money back at a later date. A joint account of this kind would avoid probate, however. In addition, if the child should subsequently withdraw the $3,000, placing the money in the child's own name in another account, the money transfer would then qualify as a tax-free gift.

Using these $3,000 annual exclusions, even over a period of years, may represent only a fractional part of a large estate. But it should be kept in mind that such tax exempt gifts would represent money taken off the top part of the estate tax bracket, possibly reducing the tax rate on all the remaining property that is to pass at the time of the estate owner's death.

And since the giving of regular annual gifts would reduce the size of the estate, there should be a corresponding reduction in the *costs of probate,* which are the costs of administering the estate. As probate fees usually run from about 5 to 8 percent of the value of the estate, this reduction should also be an appreciable saving. In addition, it may be kept in mind that parents are frequently in a higher income tax bracket than children. From the standpoint of total family income, it is often advantageous to have the income from the total of such gifts credited to the children. Unless the children have considerable income, their additional income tax from the gift may be relatively insignificant.

It is not necessary for the giver to file a federal gift tax return if the value of the gift is within the $3,000 annual exclusion. But in those cases where the spouse consents and the gift is worth from $3,000 to $6,000 for the year, a federal gift tax return must be filed, even though no tax is due.

To qualify for this annual exclusion, the gift must be a present interest in property. The person receiving it must be given either immediate possession, use, or enjoyment of the property. This means that if the parents reserve a life estate, giving the remainder interest in a summer home to their children, the transaction will not qualify as a gift in the tax-free category. Accordingly, a federal gift tax return must be filed and the appropriate tax paid on this transaction.

If a child receiving gifts is a minor, the gift can be placed in trust. In this situation, the trust is a separate legal entity, and the income from trust funds could accumulate until needed, although income accumulation in a trust can cause legal problems under some circumstances. Frequently, a gift in trust is set up by grandparents for the education of a grandchild. Such a trust makes it possible to establish ground rules for the use and eventual disposition of the gift—to permit the giver to retain some measure of control.

JOINT PROPERTY OWNERSHIP AND THE FEDERAL GIFT TAX

Ordinarily a purchase of property registered in joint ownership (other than by a husband and wife) is regarded by federal tax authorities as a gift, provided the purchasers did not contribute equally in value to the purchase price. The size of the gift in this situation is legally measured by the proportionate life ex-

pectancies of the two joint tenants. Consequently, if you paid for
the entire price of a home and put title in the name of a son and
yourself, the value of the gift to the son would be somewhat
greater than half of the value of the home. This would be because
of the son's longer life expectancy.

However, there is an exception to this rule if the joint
purchase is made by a husband and wife. A provision in federal
tax laws, enacted in 1954, excludes an automatic presumption
that there was a gift here. The federal law does not construe this
transaction as a gift from one spouse to the other, unless the
purchaser elects to have it so regarded for tax purposes at that
time. If not treated as a gift at the time of purchase, however, it
will be treated as a gift if the wife shared in the proceeds in the
event of a subsequent sale. The gift would be any value beyond
the wife's proportionate share of what she contributed to the
original purchase price.

GIFT TAX
MARITAL DEDUCTION

There is a federal gift tax marital deduction, in addition to
the annual gift tax exclusion of $3,000. The marital deduction
provides a deduction of 100 percent of the first $100,000 in gifts
to a spouse during one's lifetime. After the $100,000 deduction
is allowed, a gift valued from $100,000 to $200,000 is fully
taxed on the excess over $100,000. For all marital gifts over
$200,000 there is a marital deduction of 50 percent, regardless of
amount.

Therefore, on a marital gift of $400,000, the first $100,000
would be tax-free; the second $100,000 would be completely
taxable; and half of the portion of the gift from $200,000 to
$400,000 would be exempt from taxation.

ELECTING TO TREAT JOINT OWNERSHIP AS A GIFT FROM ONE SPOUSE TO THE OTHER

We have already noted some of the problems that may face a married couple owning property jointly. If the husband dies first, it can be anticipated that the jointly owned property will be taxed as though owned 100 percent by him. But it may be possible to shift part of this tax burden through use of the gift tax marital deduction. In effect, the law provides that the purchase can be treated as one-half ownership by the husband through purchase, and one-half ownership by the wife through a lifetime gift from the husband.

This election to treat the joint ownership as partly financed by the husband's gift will frequently be advantageous, both in the avoidance of estate taxes and income taxes that may fall due. This advantage comes about because there may be little or no federal gift tax to pay in arranging this transaction. For example, a husband and wife may obtain joint registration of the ownership of a home costing $90,000. The couple made a down payment of $12,000 and agreed to pay the balance of $78,000 in twenty annual installments of $3,900 plus interest.

The $12,000 down payment was made entirely from the husband's earnings, and he elected to treat half of the down payment and half of the annual payments as a gift to his wife. The gift of the down payment of $6,000 was tax exempt (for gift tax purposes) because of the $3,000 annual exclusion and in part to the marital deduction on the first $100,000 in the marital exemption. The annual payments of $3,900 represent regular gifts of half that amount ($1,950 plus interest) to the wife. Again, no gift tax would be payable, since the annual payment would be below the annual gift tax exclusion.

Because of the $100,000 marital gift tax deduction and the $3,000 annual exclusion, even larger house payments could have been contracted for without the payment of federal gift taxes. If the house should later be sold for $150,000, the money received from the sale could be split. The money derived from the appreciation in value would not be a gift, provided the gifts from the husband had been sufficient to "pay" for half of the down payment and half the annual payments. If a couple does elect to treat a joint ownership purchase as a gift, this must be done by filing a federal gift tax return for the calendar quarter in which the election was made. This return, of course, lists the amount of the gift. Federal law requires that this return be filed, even though no gift tax may be due, because it is under the annual exclusion of $3,000.

14

Charitable Bequests As Tax Deductions

DETERMINATION OF WHAT IS A CHARITY

A charitable bequest is one method that may be used to cut down the amount of a gross estate subject to federal estate taxation. Section 2055 of the Internal Revenue Code of 1954 provides that there is no restriction on the amount of gifts that may qualify as charitable deductions under the federal estate tax law.

Keep in mind, however, that some states do place limits on the percentage of your estate that may be given to charity. These statutory limits apply if there are specific heirs living, or if the will was executed within a short period immediately before your death, covered by so-called "fear of hell" statutes. They are described in Chapter 4, under "Disinheritance; Bequests to Other Than Ordinary Heirs." Accordingly, the amount of your gifts to charity could be limited by the laws of the state where you live.

One of the basic problems in deducting the amount of your gifts is in ascertaining whether or not a particular bequest qualifies under the definition of a *charity* as required by federal law. The mere fact that you give away your money, in itself, is not sufficient. For the recipient of a gift to qualify as a *deductible charity,* the courts usually require that the giving must be entirely gratuitous and untainted by any possibility of private gain. It must be to a cause designed for the improvement of physical, spiritual, mental, or social conditions, or for philanthropic or humanitarian purposes. The ultimate recipients must constitute either the community as a whole, or an unascertainable and unidentifiable portion or group of individuals.[1]

To be tax deductible, the money or property must be given to a public charity, and not to a private charity or private individual. If you made a donation of $1,000 to your down-and-out roommate from college, it would not qualify as tax deductible, since the legal test is not satisfied by singling out a specific individual. The interpretation of the courts and the Internal Revenue Service is that the identity of recipients must be undetermined, although the giver can specify that the gift is to go to a specified group or class of individuals.

Two actual cases illustrate how this may work. In one instance, a gift was made to a trust to provide scholarships for student nurses. In the second case, a gift was made to a trust to provide relief for the needy. In both cases, the giver specified that preference was to be given to relatives or friends of the giver. Both gifts were upheld as deductible charitable bequests, since only the class of the beneficiaries was specified.

[1]Andrews v. YMCA of Des Moines, 284 N. W. 186; Krause v. Peoria Housing Authority, 19 N. E. 2d 193; Continental Illinois National Bank and Trust v. Harris, 194 N. E. 250.

The federal law states that a corporation does not qualify as a *charity* unless it is:

organized and operated exclusively for religious, charitable, scientific, literary, or educational purposes, including the encouragement of art and the prevention of cruelty to children or animals, no part of the net earnings of which inures to the benefit of any private stockholder or individual, and no substantial part of the activities of which is carrying on propaganda, or otherwise attempting to influence legislation, and which does not participate in, or intervene in (including the publishing or distribution of statements), any political campaign, on behalf of any candidate for public office.[2]

A lodge or fraternal order need not be founded solely for charitable purposes in order to qualify as the beneficiary of a tax free charitable donation. An outright gift to the Shrine lodge, with no restrictions or limitations, would not be allowable. But a gift would qualify as a deductible charity if the bequest was to be used only for the support and maintenance of the Shriner's Crippled Children's Hospital.

CHARITABLE REMAINDERS AS DEDUCTIBLE

The so-called *charitable remainder trust* is an additional tool that the estate planner may use to reduce the taxable gross estate. In a typical situation of this kind, a residuary clause in the testator's will created a testamentary trust which would pay income to the maker's sister for life. The remainder would then pass to the March of Dimes on the sister's death. This would allow the deceased's estate a deduction for the value of the remainder that

[2]Internal Revenue Code of 1954, Sec. 2055.

would eventually pass to the March of Dimes. The value of this remainder would be calculated by obtaining the present discounted value of the gift. This value can be ascertained by computation of the worth, arrived at by taking into account the beneficiary's life expectancy, calculated from life insurance actuarial tables.[3]

In one sense, the creation of this charitable remainder trust would work for the benefit of the testator's (creator's) estate, since the deduction allowed for the charitable gift would increase the size of the trust principal from which the sister would draw income. Over the years, this type of charitable remainder trust has continued to be used. This use has led to considerable litigation in the courts, however, in instances where trust terms permitted the trustees to invade the principal of the trust, allowing variable payments of both principal and interest to be made to the income beneficiary.

In 1969, federal tax laws specified that thereafter there would be no income tax, gift tax, or estate tax deductions permitted for a charitable remainder trust unless the trust fell into one of three categories. These three categories were listed as an annuity trust, a unitrust, or a pooled income fund. The law then defined a *charitable remainder annuity trust* as one under which a set amount of not less than 5 percent of the trust principal is to be paid annually to the beneficiary or beneficiaries. The law also defined a *unitrust* as one in which a designated percentage of the annually valued principal, never less than 5 percent, is to be paid to the beneficiaries. A *pooled income fund* was described as a fund established under technical rules that do not apply to the purpose of this book (under Rev. Rul. 72–196).

The result is that there is some chance your gift through a charitable remainder trust may not be upheld as an allowable estate tax deduction if the trustees have complete discretion to invade the trust principal for the benefit of the income beneficiary.

[3]See Treasury Regulations, Sec. 2512–9, Table A-2.

III

Trusts As Tools in Estate Planning

15

Trusts—
Their Nature
And Makeup

HOW A TRUST IS SET UP
AND OPERATES

For many years, the public's impression of a *trust* was a combination of firms or corporations, formed together by some sort of legal agreement. But gradually, another kind of trust came into common usage—the so-called *personal trust,* usually set up by individuals. Of the tools that are available in estate planning, it is most likely that a trust is the least understood and least appreciated of these devices. Since many individuals do not understand trusts, they therefore take the approach that "trusts must be for somebody else."

In simplest terms, a *personal trust* is the holding of property—either personal property, real estate, or any other kind of interest—for the benefit of such individuals or institutions for which the trust was created.

Basically, a *trust* is a legal arrangement by which money or property is given to a new legal entity, called the *trust.* This money or property is to be administered by an individual or institution such as a trust company or bank, called the *trustee.* This fund or property is administered for the best interests of a designated beneficiary. You, yourself, may be the beneficiary of your own trust, although the beneficiary is usually another individual or an organization. A trustee who accepts the responsibility for handling the trust fund is required to account for all money or assets received, and will be liable in a civil lawsuit for mishandling or for embezzlement. The beneficiary is entitled to receive the income or money obtained from the property or investments, as set out in the terms of the trust. The individual who puts up the money or property for the funding of the trust is called the *creator* or *trustor.* This individual may also be called the *grantor,* the *settlor,* the *donor,* or the *founder* of the trust. More than one trustee may be selected and used. In addition, *alternate* or *substitute trustees* may be appointed, to take over in the event the original trustee is deceased or otherwise unable to perform.

The money or property that is given to the trust is called the *trust fund,* the *principal,* the *corpus,* the *res,* or the *body of the trust.* This trust fund may consist of real estate investments, stocks or bonds, cash, insurance, or even a going business. The assets in the trust fund may change from time to time, depending on the investments made by the trustee and depending on the restrictions placed on the trustee, as well as instructions given to that official.

The trust is usually set up by a legal document called a *trust agreement* or trust indenture. The person establishing the trust can use it for any legitimate purpose that he or she chooses. And there are no restrictions on a trust so long as the purposes are legal and the trust does not violate limiations set up by state law. Laws concerning trusts do vary from jurisdiction to jurisdiction, however. These laws are basically concerned with placing some limitations on the powers of the trustee and on the period of time that property can be held subject to the trust.

Long ago, English courts developed the principle called *the rule against perpetuities*. This is a legal principle designed to keep some of the old lords from eventually tying up all available property in England in their estates. This rule against perpetuities was adopted in U.S. law and is followed in all states in this country, except Idaho and Wisconsin. The rule against perpetuities provides that property cannot be owned for longer than that of a life of a person already existing, plus an additional twenty-one years. In other words, any attempt to pass on property, either through a regular deed or through a trust arrangement, is limited by this rule. Prior to the adoption of the rule, some of the English lords had set up a series of life estates to their heirs, to the heirs of their heirs, and to the heirs of the heirs of their heirs, in an indefinite chain. This was done, so that the family property would never be lost.

State laws also usually provide that the trustee is personally liable in a lawsuit if the trustee does not make the type of investments specified in the trust agreement, or if the trustee invests in stocks and bonds that are not of the blue chip variety. If the trust agreement so specifies, however, the trustee may have authority for any kind of investment. The individual setting up the trust may also select the length of time that the trust is to last, provided this is not beyond the rule against perpetuities. The person establishing the trust can also select the beneficiaries, specify how much each will get and when it will be received. In addition, the trust agreement can spell out certain conditions that must be complied with by a beneficiary in order to receive the trust fund or the income from the trust fund.

Essential Requirements of a Trust

To summarize the essential requirements or elements of a trust there must be:

1. a designated beneficiary,

2. a designated trustee,

3. assets or property sufficiently identified to enable title to the property to pass to the trustee (who is the technical owner, with the beneficiary said by the courts to be the beneficial owner), and

4. an actual delivery and acceptance by the trustee of the trust fund, or indicia of title, with the intention of passing ownership to the trust assets.

The beneficiaries of a trust may be as yet unborn, or may be unknown persons at the time the trust is established. If there is no one eligible to receive the benefits of the trust, when the trust terminates, the trust may specify that certain other individuals are to receive the assets. These persons are called *remaindermen,* whether they are males or females. In addition, the trust may specify that the income for a certain number of years is to go to certain beneficiaries, and at the termination of the trust, the funds remaining are to be paid to specified remaindermen.

WHO IS REGARDED AS THE OWNER OF A TRUST?

Legally, a trust involves a unique concept—that of double-ownership. The courts say that the trustee holds the legal title to the trust property, but that the beneficiary has the beneficial or equitable interest in it. In some situations, the trustee is allowed to use or take other legal action to protect trust funds. If, however, the trustee has misused trust funds, the beneficiary is permitted to sue the trustee. This is permitted, even though the beneficiary is not party to a contract and the beneficiary is not actually the legal owner of the property. The beneficiary's equitable interest is regarded as sufficient to maintain the lawsuit.

SIZE OF A TRUST

There is no rule governing how large a trust should be. And size should vary with the purpose of the trust. The individual setting up the trust can assign practically all of that person's assets to it, or only those needed to accomplish a specific purpose. There is no minimum size for a trust; however, practicality governs. Commercial trust companies and banks frequently set a minimum of $100,000 to $200,000 in trust funds before the institution will accept responsibility for handling. The result is that a trust is sometimes regarded as an estate planning tool that is available only to the wealthy or moderately wealthy. But in many instances, you may be able to get a knowledgeable, money-wise friend or relative to handle a trust for a minimum fee or for nothing at all.

THE TRUSTEE'S RESPONSIBILITY

In most instances, the basic part of a trustee's job is to make good investments in prudent, worthwhile stocks and bonds or properties. The trustee should never take chances and should be conservative, unless the terms of the trust provides otherwise. Generally, the courts hold a trustee to the rule that investments must be conservative, must be a good quality, and diversified.

Some states have statutes that specifically make a trustee personally responsible if he or she should invest in "fly-by-night" securities. Because of the responsibilities that are involved, it is not
always easy to find someone who will serve as trustee. Another
consideration here is that many private individuals who are honest and willing simply have no background in making business
investments.

SUGGESTING A TRUST ARRANGEMENT TO THOSE YOU MAY INHERIT FROM

Concern for the use of a trust should not be limited to your
own personal estate. It may be advisable to suggest the use of a
trust to those who may leave property to you. In one recent case,
an individual had an estate of moderate size in his own right.
When this individual's father died, he inherited $250,000 from
his father's estate. Obviously, the man receiving the inheritance
did not want to give it up, but neither did he want an increase in
his own taxable estate. In addition, he was not in need of the
income that would be produced by the $250,000 inheritance
because he was already in a high income tax bracket. For the
long-term financial good of this family, it may have been preferable for the grandfather to have left the $250,000 in trust to
grandchildren, rather than to his son in an outright bequest.

USING A LAWYER TO SET UP ANY TRUST ARRANGEMENT

Setting up a trust of any type is almost always a highly
complicated matter. It should never be attempted by using a
form book or other self-help technique. A lawyer should always
be consulted.

DISTRIBUTION ARRANGEMENTS FOR TRUST FUNDS

A number of options are available for the distribution of interest or principal from trust funds. Some of these distribution methods include the following:

1. *Sprinkling Trust.* An arrangement by which the trustee distributes trust income among beneficiaries according to changing needs and individual financial situations. For example, the trustee might apportion more money to a child in college than to one who has finished school and who already has a secure business position.

2. *Spendthrift Trust.* An arrangement by which the trustee gives regular income payments to a beneficiary who is unable or unwilling to handle money properly. A trust of this kind usually permits only the payment of income and shields the trust principal from a beneficiary who is not old enough or is unable to handle financial affairs. Originally this kind of trust was set up to care for wastrels, but it could be used for the protection of senile parents or young children.

3. *Accumulation Trust.* An arrangement by which income from trust funds is allowed to accumulate, rather than to be paid out regularly to the beneficiary. The object here may be to accumulate a specific sum of money to enable the beneficiary to eventually go into business or to use for some other specific purpose. Originally, trusts of this kind were set up to effect income tax savings because the income earned by the trust principal would have been subjected to a higher rate if it had been paid to the beneficiary, rather than being allowed to accumulate. This type of dissemination has been restricted in a number of circumstances however by changes in federal tax laws. An attorney's advice should be obtained prior to considering this type of dissemination.

BASIC DIVISIONS OR TYPES OF TRUSTS

There are a number of ways in which trusts may be classified. Basically, any trust is either (1) a living trust or (2) a testamentary trust. A *living trust* is also commonly called an *inter vivos trust* (meaning a trust between living people). A *testamentary trust* takes its name from the fact that it is created in a last will and testament and therefore does not exist until the death of the creator of the trust.

Revocable and Irrevocable Trusts

A living trust is either *revocable* or *irrevocable.* If you create a trust that is revocable during your lifetime, it becomes irrevocable at the time of your death. A *testamentary trust,* set in operation at the time of your death, is of course irrevocable by the very nature of the transaction itself. A *revocable trust* is one that can be changed, amended, or closed out completely by the individual who created it. Sometimes a living trust may be set up for the benefit of the individual who established it. If you chose to do so, you could set up a trust with your own funds, naming yourself as beneficiary or one of the beneficiaries. In addition, you could serve as the trustee or one of the trustees administering this trust. While a trust of this kind may be completely legal if properly set up by your lawyer, keep in mind that the court may feel that an arrangement of this kind is an attempt to avoid some of your personal legal obligations. At any rate, the courts usually give this kind of trust more scrutiny than falls upon other types.

A living trust comes into being when the individual who created it and the trustee both sign the trust agreement, with the trustee accepting the responsibility for handling the trust funds, and with the trustee actually accepting the trust property.

Some Examples of Living (Inter Vivos) Trusts

To observe a typical living (inter vivos) trust, consider the case of Dr. Mary Heitmann, a successful pediatrician who is a divorcee without children. Because of her successful medical practice, Dr. Heitmann is not plagued with personal money concerns. She has never been interested in investing her earnings or in following investment procedures. At the same time, Dr. Heitmann does not want to become a financial burden to her aged mother and father or her brothers and sisters. Consequently, she has placed most of her assets into a living trust, with the trust department of her bank acting as trustee. One of the provisions of this trust is that she can withdraw principal if she should have serious financial needs. She holds out enough income to take care of her office expenses and her own personal needs. The rest of her money goes into the trust fund. If the doctor should become incapacitated, the trust company will use her funds to maintain her in good style. If she should develop a serious medical problem that would require extensive care, she has authority to remove some of the principal of her trust. In the event of her death, the trust company will turn over the principal of the trust fund to her nephews and nieces.

Another individual making use of a typical living, or inter vivos, trust is Warren Edwards. Mr. Edwards made approximately $2 million as an investor and real estate speculator and has been retired for a number of years. Now 75 years of age, Mr. Edwards lives alone since the death of his wife. Approximately six months ago, Mr. Edwards suffered a stroke that was classified as mild to severe. He sustained some loss of ability to speak and was crippled somewhat in the left leg. By investing a good part of his assets in a trust, he has created an arrangement for receiving a sizable monthly check from the investment of the trust principal. Mr. Edwards has always liked to travel and he still makes trips that consume three or four months before returning to the United States. With an arrangement of this kind, he is able to live without financial worries and still knows that the principal of the trust will be paid to his grandchildren upon his death. Mr. Edwards' decision to utilize a trust was based, in good part, on his knowledge of his physical condition. Doctors have informed Mr. Edwards that he may have an additional stroke at any time, due to his age and due to the fact that doctors have not been able to bring his blood pressure within acceptable limits. In the event he does sustain another stroke, Mr. Edwards fears that he may be almost completely helpless and in need of regular income and around-the-clock care. At the same time, he intends to hold on to his trust principal for eventual distribution to his heirs.

Mr. Edwards knows that if his assets were not involved in the trust, he could lose a large part of his money through his own miscalculations, especially if he suffered brain damage in the event of another stroke. The trust arrangement should continue to protect Mr. Edwards against his own inability. While none of us like to consider the possibility of becoming senile, it is a distinct possibility in the aging process.

Testamentary Trusts

It is fairly common for an individual to create a trust in his or her will, usually for the benefit of the spouse, the children, or other members of the family. In a typical trust of this kind, the trustee is instructed to pay the income to the beneficiary named by you. In addition, in a trust of this kind you can instruct the trustee to take necessary sums out of principal to handle unusual expenses that may be encountered by your beneficiaries. This type of payment is usually called *invading the principal*.

A trust of this kind comes into being when the executors of the estate distribute your assets to the trustee or trustees named in your will, or appointed by the judge of a court if your designated trustee is unable to perform.

Some Advantages and Disadvantages
of a Revocable Trust

By a *revocable trust,* we mean an inter vivos trust that can be changed, amended, or terminated at any time. The nature of this arrangement is such that the maker can change it without notice to anyone. The beneficiary originally named may be omitted at any time and a new beneficiary added, or the terms and the manner of payment may be altered. In some trusts of this kind, the creator of the trust may reserve the right to change trustees at his or her whim.

Note, however, that a revocable trust is not set up to obtain tax advantages. The person creating the trust must continue to pay taxes on the principal. This is true, even though the creator of the trust may not receive income from it.

Specific Advantages of Revocable Trusts

Some authorities on estate planning say that when the advantages of a revocable trust are completely analyzed, this arrangement may be perhaps the most useful tool available in planning money conservation.

1. *Avoiding Probate with a Revocable Trust.* Observe that a living trust does not reduce taxes, and attorney's fees are always incurred in setting up of a trust of this kind. At the same time, note that a living trust avoids the delays and costs of probate. In most jurisdictions, the cost to create a living trust is less than the cost for bond premiums and court costs required in the probate process.

2. *A Continuance of Management of Your Property.* The use of a living trust permits the continuance of a property management program, even after the death of the creator of the trust. If you should set up a trust of this kind, there is every

reasonable assurance that it will continue to termination along the lines determined by you.

3. *Privacy.* A revocable trust arrangement is a private matter, between the creator, the trustee, and the beneficiary. By using a revocable trust, you have a reasonable certainty that the details and size of your estate and the disposition made of it will not be available to the general public. This, of course, is not a matter of concern to some individuals, but there are many of us who are very sensitive about the handling of our private financial matters. In addition, in most jurisdictions, the use of a revocable trust will give your estate exemption from creditors. Property deposited in a living trust by a creator who acted in good faith, and who was solvent when the transfer was made, is generally held to be free from the claims of the creator's future creditors.

4. *Permitting Your Children to Handle Your Estate Through Use of a Living Trust.* Under the law in many jurisdictions, your children may not be legally qualified to serve as executors and trustees under a will, because the executor and/or trustee is required to live in the same state where you reside. This problem can usually be avoided if you place most of your assets in a living trust, naming one or all of your children as trustees, along with a bank located in the community where your child or children live.

5. *Testamentary Type Proof Not Required When the Estate Passes Through a Living Trust.* We have observed earlier that wills are sometimes subject to attack from disgruntled heirs. We also noted that the probate courts have strict requirements for the necessary testamentary proof required to have the will recognized as valid. Lawyers are in general agreement that inter vivos transactions are rarely upset by the courts on the claim that the creator had an unsound mind or on the existence of undue influence factors. Nor are inter vivos

transactions usually subjected to the compromise proceedings which sometimes apply to wills that are offered for probate. In short, there is little likelihood that a living trust arrangement will be upset because of claim that the trust beneficiary influenced you in an undue manner.

6. *The Flexibility of a Living Trust.* A living trust allows the creator to retain considerable flexibility in the handling of his or her estate. The creator continues to retain the right to change the trustee or trustees at any time, subject only to the fact that the trustee may not agree to serve under changed instructions. The creator can also change or add beneficiaries, or change the method of distributing trust proceeds at any time. These options enable the creator of a revocable trust to continue almost complete control.

7. *Selecting the State from Which a Revocable Trust Operates.* The creator can choose the state from which a living trust operates. This enables the creator to do business in a jurisdiction that does not have a heavy state tax on inheritances.

8. *Life Insurance Advantages of a Living Trust.* In a number of jurisdictions, life insurance is exempt from the payment of state death taxes, provided the policy is made payable to a named beneficiary or to the trustee of a living trust. It may be advantageous to have your life insurance made payable to the trustee of a living trust since the trustee or your executor can often use the cash from the life insurance policy to avoid the forced sale of a family business, the family home, or a tract of land that should be retained. There is a second advantage. If life insurance proceeds are made payable to your spouse, the proceeds may be exempt from state death taxes when you die, but upon the spouse's death, any remaining life insurance payments will be a part of the spouse's estate, subject to estate taxation. Payment to your trustee would avoid this possibility for double taxation.

Using a Living Trust in Connection with a "Pour Over" Will

Some individuals find that it is practical to create a living trust as part of an estate plan. In connection with this living trust, the creator may leave a will with a *"pour over" provision.* In an arrangement of this kind, the testator leaves a will providing that all of his or her residuary estate is to go to the trustee of a living trust, which is already in existence, so that the bulk of the estate will revert to the living trust, after all specific bequests have been satisfied. By use of this technique, most of an individual's property may go to the trustee of a living will, leaving only a small amount of property to be handled by the executor in the distribution under the will. In legal circles, this arrangement is called a *"pour over" will.* An example of a typical living revocable trust incorporated into a "pour over" type will appears in Appendix 10.

Disadvantages of a Revocable Trust

One of the most serious disadvantages to a revocable trust is that the creator-beneficiary, may become mentally muddled and revoke the trust just at the time when the trust arrangement is needed most. For example, an individual who set up a revocable trust for his or her own benefit may be in a position to sit back and have the trust administered by a professional trust company or other responsible trustee. In rare cases, however, the creator-beneficiary may become senile, suffer a mind-impairing stroke, or become otherwise mentally incapacitated, and thereafter demand the return of all properties in possession of the trustee. If the creator-beneficiary then attempts to handle his or her own financial affairs, the result could be disastrous.

THE IRREVOCABLE TRUST

An *irrevocable trust* comes into being when the creator signs away his or her right to revoke or terminate the trust, as a part of the trust agreement.

Lawyers frequently point out that the estate planner should be hesitant to utilize an irrevocable trust so long as the creator is an individual of good health and of moderate financial means. This advice may be given to any person who has not relinquished his or her active responsibilities in the business world.

But there are two good reasons why an irrevocable trust may be used. First, if properly drafted, a trust of this kind should result in savings of both estate taxes and income taxes. Secondly, the irrevocable trust possesses all of the advantages provided by the revocable trust, but the use of an irrevocable trust is much more limited. Many individuals who have less than very substantial means are not willing to lose control over their assets. Yet it is frequently beneficial in estate planning. Individuals of substantial wealth frequently use an irrevocable inter vivos transfer of funds, instead of using a will, to provide for the support, education, or comfort of non-dependent members of the family.

If an outright gift is given to a relative, there is no certainty that the relative may not quickly dispose of the gift funds. The use of an irrevocable trust is protection to the beneficiary (beneficial owner) that an outright gift cannot supply.

An irrevocable trust, as we will see in the section on taxation and trusts, can save you money on both income taxes and estate taxes.

Sprinkling Provisions

A trust with *sprinkling provisions* enables the trustee to distribute income among any in a group of beneficiaries, according to the trustee's judgment. This sprinkling arrangement may have both advantages and disadvantages.

The trustee can use the sprinkling authority to make payments to beneficiaries who are deserving or who are in greater need than other potential beneficiaries. In addition, an arrangement of this kind permits the trust income to be varied. This allows lower-bracket beneficiaries to receive more income than higher-bracket beneficiaries. As a result, the family's total income tax bill may be reduced somewhat.

In addition, the sprinkling arrangement permits the trustee to take care of unforeseen family emergencies. Realizing that an adequate flow of income would be available from the trust, some beneficiaries have given away some of their own individual assets during lifetime to minimize estate taxes.

On the other side of the picture, there is no question that the distribution of unequal amounts of trust income could lead to serious family quarrels. Another problem created by the use of a sprinkling trust provision is that beneficiaries may never be quite sure of their financial standing.

An Example of a Trust with Sprinkling Distribution

To illustrate how the sprinkling provision may be used in trust payments, consider the case of a grandfather who wanted to make sure that his grandchildren had an opportunity for a good education. The grandfather set up a trust fund, with one of his sons to act as trustee. The grandfather had ten grandchildren, although the trustee had no children of his own. The trustee was given authority to make income distribution from a fund of $300,000 to any or all of the grandchildren, based on their school achievement records, eligibility for college, apparent personal desire for education and other individual accomplishments. The trustee had sole authority to make payments to any of the grandchildren based on his assessment of individual needs and individual potential.

The trust was set up so that all funds would remain in the prinicpal until the last grandchild graduated from college or reached the age of twenty-three, whichever came last. The instructions to the trustee then provided that all remaining funds were to be shared alike by all of the grandchildren.

It eventually developed that one grandchild never attended college and that one dropped out after a short attendance. Two grandchildren received master's degrees, with help from the trust, while a third received a Ph.D. The grandchild who did not attend college expressed some resentment, but this was apparently merely a phase. Each of the grandchildren eventually received a substantial sum from the trust, and each had an opportunity for a good education, in accordance with the grandfather's wishes.

ALIMONY TRUSTS

In some instances, an alimony trust may be used as part of the financial settlement in a divorce matter. The legal requirements for a trust of this kind are usually highly technical and it would be necessary to develop such an arrangement only with the planning of a tax advisor and a lawyer.

POWER OF APPOINTMENT UNDER A TRUST

A *power of appointment,* set up under a trust, is an arrangement commonly used when you give your spouse a life estate in your property. This means that your spouse could use your property during his or her life and that it would then pass to someone else. The power of appointment is a right that falls to the widow or widower to make a selection as to who will get the property on his or her death. Typically, a trust arrangement of this kind also instructs that if the widow or widower does not use the power of appointment, which is called making an *election,* then the property reverts to the creator's children or other heirs.

Basically, a power of appointment right is included in a trust because of unusual family situations. For example, the creator may feel that one of his or her children may need more than the others, or one potential heir may be more deserving than others. The power of appointment right gives considerable flexibility to the way in which property may be disposed of in an individual family.

There is a potential problem here, when you include the right of a power of appointment in your will. So long as the creator provides that the individual holding the power can choose the eventual heirs among the creator's children, grandchildren, or some other specific class of individuals, there should be no federal tax problem. The legal test is that if the person who holds the power of appointment cannot exercise it for his or her own benefit or for the benefit of his or her estate, the trust property will not be taxable in his or her estate under the federal estate tax. If an appointment is not made by the individual holding the power of appointment, the person designated to take the property is known as the *taker in default of appointment.*

Stated in other terms, there are two types of powers of appointment: One of these is known legally as a "general power of appointment," and the other type is called a "special power of appointment." Although there are some exceptions, a *general power of appointment* is usually defined by the courts as a power exercisable in favor of the deceased, his or her estate, his or her creditors, or any creditors of his or her estate. Those assets or properties that are subject to the general power are taxed in the deceased's estate, whether or not the power could be exercised during the deceased's lifetime or in his or her will. The courts define a *special power of appointment* as a power to appoint among a restricted class of persons that does not include the deceased (decedent), his or her estate, his or her creditors, or the creditors of his or her estate. Restricting the power of appointment of selecting individuals within a specific class, such as "among my grandchildren," will be sufficient to insure that the property is not taxed in the estate of the person holding the power of appointment.

Undoubtedly, there may be times when an estate planner may want to use a power of appointment. Because of the technical legal requirements and problems here, a plan of this kind should be considered only in conjunction with your attorney and your tax advisor.

WHETHER YOU WANT TO CONSIDER A TRUST

Whether you want to consider the use of a trust may depend on a number of factors.

If you are leaving a substantial sum to someone in an inheritance, you may feel that the money will last forever. Properly invested and handled, a considerable sum could provide adequate income and even increase in value. But much depends on the experience, background, and personal characteristics of the beneficiary. Frequently, inexperienced individuals are unable to take care of their money and may quickly dissipate it. If property is given as an outright bequest, it may be quickly dissipated or reached by the recipient's creditors. In addition, there is the ever-present possibility that your money will fall into the hands of a second husband or children of another marriage in which you have no interest. The expenses of trust administration, the interest return that can be expected, and many other factors may enter in.

And of course, in some instances you may avoid tax or probate charges and pass on considerably more by use of a trust. Specific examples of this kind are pointed out in the section on taxation and trusts.

Whether you would want to set up a trust for yourself as beneficiary will vary, depending on your own assessment of your physical health, whether you have the ability to make investments, whether the time has come to be relieved of the investment responsibility, and your own economic position.

IV

Tax Avoidance: The Marital Deduction And Trusts To Save Money

16

The Marital Deduction

BACKGROUND
OF THE PROBLEM

Up to 1948, the federal estate tax was not applied uniformly in all states. In common law jurisdictions, all property acquired through the husband's earnings were taxed in his estate upon his death. But in a community property state, only the husband's one-half interest (his community property) was includible in his taxable gross estate. In a community property state, the surviving spouse's share of the community property was eventually taxed in her estate, but this postponement of taxation left the wife with the use of this tax money all during her lifetime. In addition,

175

both the husband and the wife owning property in community property states were allowed to claim the standard estate tax exemption when death occurred. This standard exemption was $60,000 up until 1976. The practical effect of all this was that twice the amount of the community property was exempt from the federal estate tax as that in a common law state. Obviously, this placed people in a common law state at a distinct disadvantage.

The *Internal Revenue Code of 1948* contained revisions in the federal estate tax laws, designed to bring about equality in the tax treatment of married couples, whether the couples lived in a common law or community property state.

Under the tax laws from 1948 to 1976, Section 2056 of the Internal Revenue Code permitted a husband or wife to leave a tax free marital deduction to the surviving spouse. This was accomplished by leaving up to one-half of the spouse's separate property to the surviving spouse or to make some other transfer that legally qualified. The result was that only one-half of the decedent's property was subject to the federal estate tax, just as half of the decedent's property owned as community property was taxable in a community property state.

The way the marital deduction operated from 1948 to 1976 was that a transfer of no more than one-half to the spouse was allowed. If the decedent transferred less than one-half, the marital deduction was limited to the amount of property that was actually transferred.

What Kind of Transfers Qualify As a Marital Deduction?

What kind of transaction is required for a marital deduction? Outright property interests passed to the spouse by intestacy, by right of survivorship in jointly owned property, or by life insurance contract all qualify. In addition, a revocable inter vivos trust funded with assets during the husband's lifetime also qualifies. A legal life estate and a general power of appointment[1] are also sufficient if the following technical requirements are satisfied:

1. The surviving husband or wife must be entitled to all of the income for life.

2. The income must be paid annually or by some more frequent arrangement.

3. The power of appointment must be a general power of apointment rather than a restricted power. In addition, the surviving spouse must have the authority to exercise the appointment during the spouse's lifetime or in that spouse's will.

4. This power of appointment must be useable by the spouse alone, and without any restrictions.

5. The spouse's interest must not be such that anyone else has the authority to divert the property to a person other than the spouse. In short, the trustee handling the trust involved cannot be given any discretionary power to distribute the res or corpus of the trust to anyone except the surviving spouse.

When first authorized in 1948, the marital deduction did not have much effect on small estates. However, lawyers began using some new techniques for medium to large estates, frequently setting up two separate trusts in one estate plan, with these referred to as "A" and "B" trusts. The first of these the *A trust*, was the marital deduction trust, in which the husband transferred his marital deduction into one trust fund. The second or *B trust* became known as the "family trust" or the "residuary trust." In the latter, property could be routed to any individual

---

[1]This is a general power of appointment under a trust, that is discussed in detail in the chapters on trusts.

the testator desired after the death of the spouse. To comply with
the law and Internal Revenue Service regulations, the corpus of
the marital deduction trust was required to be subject to testamentary disposition by the surviving husband or wife, and to
be available or reachable by creditors. Not having been taxed on
the death of the first spouse, the assets of the marital trust were,
of course, taxable in the estate of the surviving spouse. Note,
however, that this taxation was at beginning rates. It was also
necessary for the spouse to whom the marital deduction was made
to have absolute power to designate beneficiaries who would
eventually receive this property.

In a typical plan of this type in common law states, the
husband's will devised the family residence and other personal
items outright to his wife. After making any other specific bequests, the will set up a "formula gift" to the wife in a marital
deduction trust. This was either a formula fractional share of the
husband's residuary estate or a formula pecuniary gift. This formula fractional share of the residuary estate or formula pecuniary
gift was designed to result in conveying exactly the maximum
marital deduction, no more and no less. The lawyers drafting the
will could not simply bequest one-half the estate because, in the
fashion of those who set up tax legislation, the allowable deduction could be reached only by formula, taking into account the
specific bequests.

A typical fractional share gift of the type used in a marital
deduction will reads as follows:

> If my said wife survives me, I gave to [trustee] the following
> described fractional share of my residuary estate: The
> numerator of the fraction shall be the maximum estate tax
> marital deduction (allowable in determining the federal es-
> tate tax payable by reason of my death) minus the value for
> federal estate tax purposes of all items in my gross estate
> which qualify for said deduction and which pass or have
> passed in a form which qualifies for the estate tax marital

deduction from me to my said wife (the words "pass or have passed" shall have the same meaning as such words shall have under the provisions of the Internal Revenue Code in effect at the time of my death) under other provisions of this will, by right of survivorship with respect to jointly owned property, under settlement arrangements relating to life insurance proceeds, and otherwise that under this fractional share gift of my residuary estate (in computing the numerator, the values as finally determined for federal estate tax purpose shall control); and the denominator of the fraction shall be the value of my residuary estate (in computing the denominator, the value of my residuary estate shall be determined on the basis of the values as finally determined for federal estate tax purposes). If the numerator of the above-described fraction equals or exceeds the denominator, the entire residuary estate shall be placed in this marital deduction trust.

In the alternative, the lawyer drafting the will might use the following language for a formula pecuniary gift:

If my said wife survives me, I give to [trustee] the following: An amount equal to the maximum estate tax marital deduction (allowable in determining the federal estate tax payable by reason of my death) minus the value for federal estate tax purposes of all items in my gross estate which qualify for said deduction and which pass or have passed in a form which qualifies for the estate tax marital deduction from me to my said wife (the words "pass or have passed" shall have the same meaning as such words shall have under the provisions of the Internal Revenue Code in effect at the time of my death) under other provisions of this will, by right of survivorship with respect to jointly owned property, under settlement arrangements relating to life insurance proceeds, and otherwise than under this pecuniary bequest. In making the computations necessary to determine the amount of this pecuniary estate tax marital deduction gift, values as finally determined for federal estate tax purposes shall control.

These clauses from typical wills are of course complicated. They were both designed to make automatic adjustments that would take into account any property passing to the surviving spouse by any means that qualify for the marital deduction. This therefore includes the family home and any personal property given outright to the surviving spouse, life insurance policy proceeds, joint bank accounts, and any other kind of property.

The will's remaining provisions concerning the marital deduction trust were written to give the wife a life income interest, with a general power of appointment. If the surviving spouse had not exercised the power of appointment at the time of death, the remaining property would pass to the family trust. In drafting a will of this kind, the property left after the establishment of the marital deduction trust was placed in the "family trust." Under this second or the B trust, the surviving spouse was given a life interest and a special power to designate which of the couple's descendants would receive the remainder. If this power was not exercised, the couple's descendants would receive the property that was left at the time of the second spouse's death.

In large estates, where a designated income interest in the family trust would give the surviving spouse more income than needed, and consequently a larger income tax bill than desirable, the trustee might be given the discretionary power to transfer family trust income among the couple's descendants, or to accumulate trust income, therefore providing income tax savings.

CHANGES IN THE MARITAL DEDUCTION

The *Tax Reform Act of 1976* authorized changes related to the marital deduction. Although passed into law in 1976, this new marital deduction did not universally apply prior to January

1, 1979. As authorized since that date, the marital deduction allows you to leave to your spouse, outright or in trust with unlimited power of disposition, but free of tax in either case, one-half of your adjusted gross estate or $250,000, whichever is greater. According to the stated intent of Congress, this change in the marital deduction was not made effective immediately to allow individuals to revise existing wills to take care of the increased marital deduction, if they so desired.

In some instances, wills using the old language, or one of the old formulas for calculating the marital deduction, could face the possibility of unnecessary taxation at the time the second spouse passed on property to the couple's children. But because of the changed marital deduction, the surviving spouse may now receive more than half of the deceased mate's estate, unless that estate is of considerable value.

For example, consider the case of a couple with an estate of $425,000. Assume that the husband will die in 1981, leaving the maximum marital deduction to his wife. The wife would then receive the entire estate tax-free. The maximum marital deduction of $250,000 would exempt that part of the estate, leaving a balance of $175,000 subject to tax. This balance can be covered by the available estate tax credit for 1981, leaving all of the couple's money to the widow. If the widow then dies with an estate of the same size, her estate may have to pay as much as $83,300 in taxes when the property eventually passes to the couple's children.

Stated in other terms, there appear to be two possible results for estate holders in the $150,000 to $500,000 range.

1. It may be possible to leave the entire estate of a husband to the widow tax free, because of the increased marital deduction and the current estate tax credit.

2. If, however, the basic objection of the estate plan is to pass on as much as possible to the couple's children, then the use of the increased marital deduction may result in a larger

total tax bill when the estate is finally given to the children or other heirs.

In many instances, the eventual estate tax burden paid by a married couple will be less if their estates are balanced, because assets concentrated in one estate are subject to higher tax rates. Two estates of $500,000 pay a total tax of $217,600, whereas one estate of $1,000,000 pays nearly $300,000.

To illustrate, the husband dies during 1981 and his estate of $1,000,000 is passed to his wife. For her part, the widow has no assets other than the inheritance from the husband.

	Husband's Estate at Death	*Wife's Estate at Death*
Value of estate	$1,000,000	$1,000,000
Marital deduction	$ 500,000	none
Taxable estate	$ 500,000	$1,000,000
Federal estate tax	$ 108,000	$ 298,000

As the surviving spouse, the widow cannot claim a marital deduction. Consequently, her separate federal estate tax is significantly larger than that of the husband.

If two trusts—the A-B trusts—are set up and 50 percent of his estate is passed to the widow in the marital deduction trust (the A trust) and 50 percent to their children or other heirs in the family trust (B trust), the tax on the widow's estate would be only on the part owned by her (the $500,000 marital deduction). The widow would still be able to draw interest from the second trust without having additional taxes levied against her estate. The tax on the husband's estate would be $108,000, in any event. If the husband set up the A-B trust arrangement, the widow's tax would be reduced from $298,000 (levied on the entire $1 million) to the sum of $108,000. This would make a total tax savings through use of the trusts of $190,000 (the difference between the tax of $298,800 on an estate of $1 million and a tax of $108,000 on an estate of $500,000).

In most instances then, the benefit of the estate tax marital deduction will be greatest when the surviving spouse is the one with the smaller estate. Obviously, in a situation of this kind, estate planning should be directed toward balancing the taxable estates of the two spouses.

In some instances, too, consideration should be given to the possibility of reducing estate taxation by using the gift tax marital deduction, as described in the section on the federal gift tax. That deduction exempts the first $100,000 of qualifying transfers from the federal gift tax, effectively removing assets from the estate of the spouse that contains the greater assets. If the wife predeceases the husband, leaving a minimum in her estate, then the husband would incur federal estate tax liability of $298,800 on an estate of $1 million. If the husband had seen fit to make a marital deduction gift of $100,000 to the wife before her death, then no gift tax would be liable on this $100,000 amount. The effect of the gift would be to reduce the husband's estate to $900,000 that would be subject to tax. This tax would amount to $249,800, a savings of $39,000 that would accrue by giving the $100,000 gift to the wife. This assumes that the wife's property passed to the couple's children, rather than reverting back to the husband.

JOINT OWNERSHIP BY BUYERS OTHER THAN MARRIED COUPLES MAY BE SUBJECT TO GIFT TAX

No marital deduction is permitted on gifts from an individual other than a spouse. But as we have seen previously, a husband and wife can elect to split one of the spouse's gifts, so that an exemption of $6,000 can be made to any individual without tax. Consequently, an original purchase by a father and daughter as joint tenants will involve a taxable gift unless they contribute jointly.

A great number of tax problems arise in switching from single ownership to joint ownership, or from joint ownership to single. Whether the joint owners are married, and whether the property is located in a common law or community property state is, of course, also of definite significance.

The treatment in this chapter outlines only a few of the more common problems and techniques that relate to federal gift taxation. Because of the interplay of complex tax problems and property relationships, everyone should employ a local lawyer at the time property is purchased. This is in addition to the need to use the lawyer's counsel to understand obligations and commitments you must make in completing the purchase, and in understanding legal relations for you and your wife in the future use and enjoyment of the property.

Capital Gains Taxes—Due After Selling Off Inherited Property

If you have an item that costs you $3,000 or less, we have observed that you could give it to someone during your lifetime as a tax exempt gift. If it is a block of stock, the beneficiary must pay income tax on the dividends received after accepting the present. If this gift is something that the beneficiary keeps, there will be no tax liability so long as he or she continues to own it. If, however, the $3,000 gift increases in value and the beneficiary sells it for $6,000, the recipient would have to pay a capital gains tax, on an increase of $3,000.

Therefore, in choosing a gift for someone, it may be preferable to select something having a cost basis that was roughly equivalent to current market value. This, of course, would avoid subjecting the beneficiary to payment of much tax (capital gains tax). If you do own property of that kind, you may want to consider giving it to someone who may never want to part with it or giving it to someone who is likely to remain in a comparatively low income tax bracket. If your estate owns some stocks that are selling below what you paid for them, it may be good planning to take the capital loss by selling the stock, making a gift of the funds realized from the sale. This is especially true if you are in a high income tax bracket at the time.

One of the executor's or administrator's problems in settling an estate may be to arrive at values of the deceased's assets that will be approved by the probate courts. These values may be needed to figure capital gains taxes, based on the sale of assets or property.

Prior to the *Tax Reform Act of 1976 (TRA),* all inherited assets were taxed on the basis of their worth at the time of the owner's death. Under the *Tax Reform Act of 1976,* the value of the assets owned on December 31, 1976 is first ascertained (this is the arbitrary date set by law for these calculations). In the formula used, the proportion of growth prior to December 31, 1976 is figured as a fraction of the overall growth. This is the basic part of the computation, with slight variances.

For example, a collector bought an antique car for $60,000 on December 31, 1971. The collector kept the car until his death in 1977, and it was sold by the executor for $90,000 on December 31, 1978. The overall appreciation on the antique car was $30,000. It was owned for five years prior to December 31, 1976, and it was owned for one year thereafter. The tax is figured as a fraction of five years over a total of six years. The capital gain is therefore 5/6 of the overall appreciation of $30,000.

USE OF THE MARITAL DEDUCTION

Should the marital deduction be used to reduce the wife's taxes or those of the couple's children? Since the marital deduction first became available to taxpayers, the basic emphasis in estate planning has often been not to save federal taxes on the death of the first spouse, but rather to reduce the combined tax bill paid by the two spouses jointly.

Since 1948, marital deduction formula clauses have usually been worded with a view toward saving taxes on the death of the second spouse. The lawyer drafting wills or trusts of this kind usually attempted to avoid overqualifying the marital bequest in the estate of the first to die. In short, the estate planner attempted to balance the value of the two spouses' estates. This was on the idea that if more of the marital deduction was used than necessary to make the estates of equal size, then the second spouse would eventually pay more taxes. As a result, estate planners took the approach that the testators should simply utilize enough of the marital deduction so that assets in each estate would be reduced to equal amounts.

This approach is commendable if the couple hiring the lawyer intend to pass on as much as possible to their children, following the death of the second spouse. Normally, the client that the lawyer is working for in a situation of this kind is the husband. Without giving much thought to the client's objectives, these attorneys have been increasing the taxes payable by their client in order to eventually save money for the client's beneficiaries. Stated in other terms, some attorneys and estate planners have been concentrating solely on the amount of taxes being saved without evaluating who is saving this money. A thorough estate planner should feel obligated to his or her clients to note that the money being saved is not for the clients' immediate benefit, but for the benefit of the clients' children, grandchildren, or other beneficiaries.

THE MARITAL DEDUCTION IN COMMUNITY PROPERTY STATES

Before the passage of the *Tax Reform Act of 1976,* no marital deduction was allowed for estates consisting solely of community property. This was changed, however, and the new law makes a partial marital deduction available to estates made up partly or wholly of community property. Under the new rules, the $250,000 amount is adjusted in situations where the deceased owned community property at death, so that the parity provided under prior law between common law property and community property law states is continued.

The special rule for figuring the adjusted gross estate is calculated as follows: From the total value of the gross estate, the following figure is subtracted—

1. the value of community property held at the time of death; plus

2. the value of property transferred by the deceased during his or her life, provided the property was held as community property at the time of the transfer; plus

3. the amount receivable as life insurance proceeds under policies on the deceased's life, to that extent that the insurance was purchased with premiums or other consideration paid out of community property; plus

4. the sum obtained by this calculation.

$$\frac{\text{Gross Estate} - \text{Community Property}}{\text{Entire Gross Estate}} \times \begin{array}{l}\text{Sec. 2053 \& Sec.}\\ \text{2054 Deductions}\\ \text{(under Fed. Tax}\\ \text{Code).}\end{array}$$

To ascertain the marital deduction for estates of individuals dying after 1976 while holding community property, first determine the adjusted gross estate by using steps (1) through (4) of the calculations set out. Then make the adjustment to the alternative $250,000 ceiling. The marital deduction ceiling is the greater of the reduced alternative ceiling, or 50 percent of the reduced adjusted gross estate. Note, that this formula will not increase the marital deduction already allowed for estates valued at over $500,000. It is obvious, then, that the new adjustment is advantageous only for estates of small to moderate size.

Tax authorities point out that community property estates of small to medium size have benefited by this formula to the same extent that small- and medium-sized estates have benefited by the increased marital deduction in common law states, as introduced by the *Tax Reform Act of 1976.*

DISCLAIMING INHERITANCE TO INCREASE THE WIFE'S MARITAL DEDUCTION

Under the law and regulations followed by the Internal Revenue Service, heirs can disclaim their inheritance. If the heirs are children of the deceased, there are some circumstances where the wife's financial position may be benefited considerably if the children disclaim some or all of their inheritance. This benefit to the wife would accrue in situations where the husband did not leave the full amount of the marital deduction. By disclaiming their inheritance in favor of their mother (surviving spouse), the marital deduction would be increased and the taxes on the father's estate would be reduced.

THE MARITAL DEDUCTION AT SIMULTANEOUS DEATH OF HUSBAND AND WIFE

If the husband and wife are both killed in a common disaster, it may be legally difficult to claim a marital deduction. Some states permit a paragraph in a will that includes a written assumption that the wife lived longer and therefore survived the husband. In states where this type of inclusion is permitted in the will, the wife's heirs can claim a marital deduction if both the husband and wife were killed in the same accident.

SKIPPING THE MARITAL DEDUCTION IF SPOUSE HAS CHILDREN BY PRIOR MARRIAGE

In some instances, the marital deduction will be available to a surviving wife through a trust. In some instances of this kind, the wife may have children by a prior marriage and the husband may not be desirous of leaving his funds to them. If the husband is unwilling to give the wife the power of appointment by her will of one-half of the husband's taxable estate, then the husband should ignore the marital deduction will, no matter how much may be saved on the federal estate tax.

17

Trusts and
Tax Avoidance

Undoubtedly many individuals would feel a need for estate planning, even if there were no tax savings that could result. Such
individuals would want to leave behind plans and guidelines
concerning how they want their property distributed. But tax
savings, alone, are a powerful incentive to almost anyone who
accumulates any sizeable amount of money.

This section is concerned with trusts and with how trusts are
used as one of the basic tools of the estate planner in tax
avoidance. In the section on trusts, it was observed that tax
benefits cannot be obtained from the use of a revocable trust.
Accordingly, we are concerned here with irrevocable trusts.

TAX CREDIT WHEN DEATH OF SECOND SPOUSE FOLLOWS CLOSELY ON DEATH OF FIRST

One of the troublesome aspects of estate taxation is that a couple's property may be taxed twice. If a husband leaves everything to his wife, at her death everything that she passes to the children or other beneficiaries will be taxable. In effect, then, the couple is taxed twice.

Tax credits come into play here, if the death of the second spouse follows closely on the death of the first. This credit graduates downward, decreasing with the number of years that one spouse outlives the other. For example, if the wife outlived the husband by ten years, the property she leaves at her death is fully taxable. However, if the husband had died only one year prior to the wife, the tax credit allowed would be considerable. The percentage of credit allowed in successive deaths of spouses within a short period appears in Appendix 11.

THE IRREVOCABLE TRUST

If an irrevocable trust is properly drafted, it may bring about savings in both income and estate taxes. When you make this kind of transfer, you retain no strings of any kind and are not able to control the property in the future. Since control is lost, you should weigh a transfer of this kind very carefully.

If you set up an irrevocable trust and it produces income, you will not be required to include this income in your income tax, provided that all these requirements are met.

1. This income is not received by you.

2. This income is not used to support one of your children or someone that you are legally obliged to support.

3. This income is not used to satisfy one of your legal obligations.

4. This income is not accumulated for your spouse or you.

5. This income is not used to pay the premiums due on your life insurance or on your spouse's life insurance.

In the usual situation of this kind, the trust would have been set up for the benefit of some member of your family, so funds can be retained in the family circle. The income tax savings comes about because income is diverted from a high-bracket taxpayer to a beneficiary of the trust who is a low-bracket taxpayer or who does not pay income taxes at all.

In creating a trust of this kind, estate tax savings can be anticipated by transferring underlying assets to the trust. It must be emphasized, however, that there is an estate tax savings only if control is not retained by the individual who created the trust. The creator or donor cannot retain any right to income or any power to amend or alter the trust, or in any way control the use and enjoyment of the property. At the same time, the creator can serve as a trustee but the power given as trustee must not go beyond those powers that any other regular trustee would have to oversee proper investments and to safeguard the property. The creator-trustee would not be allowed any power which could modify or change the beneficiaries' interests. Nor could the creator retain the right to vote any stock that the creator transferred into the trust fund.

One way to avoid double taxation of the couple's property would be to set up an irrevocable trust where: (1) your spouse receives the income for life, and (2) the property goes to your children on your spouse's death. This is an example from a common-law state.

In a somewhat similar situation, suppose a husband and wife owned community property worth $350,000. If the first spouse dies after 1981, no federal estate tax would be due. This is because the community property owned by each spouse would be valued at $175,000. The tax credit allowable in 1981 ($47,000) would exempt the $175,000 on which an estate tax would otherwise be due. This $47,000 is the credit allowed toward the federal estate tax, as figured by the method shown in using the tax table set out in Chapter 12 and Appendix 9. This credit of $47,000 will cancel out the tax otherwise due on an estate amounting to $175,000 ($47,000).

In the usual situation, where one spouse leaves everything to the other, no federal estate tax would be due on the community property owned by the first to die. However, the second spouse to die would have an estate valued at $350,000 (the husband's one-half, $175,000 and the wife's one-half $175,000, totaling $350,000). Assuming that the husband dies first, as is usually the case, the tax of $53,000 could be avoided through use of a trust. (This figure of $53,000 is also the tax figured from the chart in Chapter 12 or in Appendix 9, under the *Tax Reform Act of 1976.*)

The trust could be set up as an irrevocable living trust or created as a testamentary trust in the husband's will. Such a trust would be for the benefit of the wife and would give her a life estate in the husband's one-half of the community property. This means that she could receive the income from this property and in addition, the trust could be designed so that the wife could invade the principal if needed. The trust could be set up so that the property passed to the couple's children, grandchildren, or other heirs at the termination of the wife's life estate. Since the wife would not own the property in the husband's trust under an arrangement of this kind, her estate would not be taxed on it, and her estate would therefore be liable only for her one-half of the community property (valued at $175,000). Since the tax allowance of $47,000 would be sufficient to exempt an estate of $175,000, under the terms of the combined gift and estate tax exemption, this amount would also be exempt from tax in the wife's estate. The eventual result of the use of the trust would be that the children or other eventual heirs would be saved a tax bill of $53,000.

Note that estate planners frequently use two trusts in a situation similar to those in the last two cases. These are sometimes referred to by legal planners as A and B trusts. The first of these is sometimes called a *marital deduction trust*. In effect, this is usually a testamentary trust designed to permit the surviving spouse to take advantage of the marital deduction. The second trust is a trust of that segment of the estate which is outside the marital deduction and on which estate taxes will be payable.

Consider another case of a grandfather whose wife had predeceased him. The grandfather had only one child, a daughter, who had three grandchildren. Suppose the grandfather created an irrevocable living trust in 1981, by contributing $178,000 in securities to the trust fund. The trust agreement would provide that the daughter was to receive all of the trust income during her life. Thus $3,000 of the trust principal would qualify as a gift, for which the grandfather would be able to claim the $3,000 annual exclusion under the gift tax law. By subtracting this exclusion of $3,000, the taxable principal was cut down to $175,000. The unified allowable credit of $47,000 (for the year 1981) would cancel out the tax due on the remaining $175,000. Accordingly, there would be no tax of any kind due on the transaction involved in setting up the trust. In the actual case involved here, the grandfather lived an additional ten years. By that time, the trust principal had appreciated and was worth $350,000 at the time of the creator's death.

One of the consequences of the trust was that the grandfather had removed the income from his own property, to income that was paid by his daughter. Since the grandfather had considerable income already, and the daughter had no appreciable income, there was an income tax savings to the family that continued year after year.

In addition, only $175,000 was reported in the grandfather's estate as a taxable transfer. The difference of $175,000 included the $3,000 gift exclusion and $172,000 in funds that had not been subjected to estate taxation. If we followed this case to its conclusion, after twenty-five years of existence the trust fund had appreciated to a value of $700,000. On the daughter's death, this $700,000 was subject to estate taxation as though it was part of her estate, as a generation-skipping transfer. But note that there were three grandchildren who were the eventual heirs, and there is a $250,000 individual exemption for each of the three grandchildren. These three exemptions, totaled together, amounted to $750,000 which was less than the $700,000 taxable under the daughter's estate. The $700,000 therefore passed to the grandchildren tax-free.

Obviously, the creator of a trust usually needs to have a considerable amount of money available. By using an irrevocable trust, a gift exclusion, and the $250,000 exclusion for grandchildren, the grandfather accomplished a great deal. He reduced his own income taxes, provided regular income for his daughter, and passed $700,000 to his combined grandchildren with an original investment of $175,000.

AVOIDING THE SO-CALLED GRANTOR-TRUSTEE TRAP IN IRREVOCABLE TRUSTS

Usually, the creator or grantor of an irrevocable trust names a close friend or relative as trustee. This selection is made so that the creator will be assured that trust assets will be managed according to the creator's preferences.

Although the trust is irrevocable, the Internal Revenue Service has ruled that the trust funds are taxable in the estate of the creator, if the creator reserves the right to substitute himself or herself as trustee, accordingly, the creator of an irrevocable trust must completely give up the ownership and control of the trust funds if the estate tax consequences are to be avoided.

THE REVERSIONARY TRUST— COMMONLY KNOWN AS A CLIFFORD TRUST

A reversionary trust is a helpful tool in saving money through the technique sometimes called *income tax shifting.* In this device, your funds are shifted in ownership to a trust that will benefit a relative or someone else you desire to help, an individual in a low-income bracket. Eventually, the funds in this trust will revert back to you. If you should die in the meantime, the funds will continue in possession of the trust, for the benefit of your beneficiary, or will revert back to your estate.

There are specific legal rules for the creation of a trust of this kind. It must last for at least ten years and a day, unless the creator dies earlier. The purpose of the trust must be one that is not a required legal obligation that must be performed by the creator. For example, the creator could not set up a trust of this kind to provide income for one of his or her children that he or she is already legally obligated to educate, according to state law. The creator must actually give up control and ownership of the trust fund and income, for the period of the trust.

By complying with these legal requirements, the individual in a high income tax bracket may shift the income to a beneficiary in a low tax bracket, or to someone who may not even pay income tax at all.

To illustrate how this works, a doctor in an eastern city had

a highly profitable medical practice. Due to family responsibilities, the doctor and his wife furnished support to both the
doctor's mother and his mother-in-law. Neither of these depen-
dents had any outside source of income. Setting aside good common stocks that he placed into a reversionary trust, the doctor
created an income for his mother for about $12,000 a year. He
also took similar funds and set them up in a second reversionary
trust for his mother-in-law. Trust income provided both his
widowed mother and his widowed mother-in-law with sufficient
income. Both of these widows were above sixty-five years of age
and had extra deductions because of age. Each beneficiary paid
little income tax because she had no other means of support. For
his part, the doctor was relieved of paying income tax on $25,000
a year, which sum he would have normally expended in support
of the mother and mother-in-law. Since the doctor was already in
a very high income tax bracket, his savings on state and federal
income tax were considerable, year after year.

There is one caution that should be observed here. Legally,
parents are required to furnish money for the education of their
own children. If a reversionary trust is set up for this purpose, it
should be done so only after careful legal research of local state
laws. In one recent instance, a federal court upheld the legality of
a reversionary trust which had been established by a father to
provide extra educational and cultural facilities for his children.
The court was convinced here that the purpose of the trust was to
provide education and benefits that were beyond the educational
obligations normally required of a parent.

There is no question, however, that a reversionary or Clifford trust, may be used by grandparents or other relatives, except
the mother and father, who have no legal obligation to furnish
education to the beneficiaries.

Much litigation in the federal courts involves trusts of this
type. Generally the problem has revolved around the fact that the
creator was reluctant to give up the management and control of
the money or stocks used to finance the trust. So when the trust

instrument was created, the creator was inclined to retain powers or to appoint a trustee who was not completely independent—someone such as a brother or a wife. When a trust arrangement of this kind comes to the attention of the Internal Revenue Service, there is a good likelihood that it may be contested in court.

The federal courts say that unless power and control over the trust fund is relinquished, the donor (creator) has not set up a valid, income-shifting device for income tax purposes.

THE FEDERAL TAX ON GENERATION-SKIPPING TRUSTS

As a part of the *Tax Reform Act of 1976,* Congress created a new tax on the transfer of money or assets that is distinct and apart from the federal estate tax and the federal gift tax. This is known as the tax on generation-skipping transfers and it applies to both inter vivos trusts or living trusts, and testamentary trusts, as well as any transfer arrangement drafted or designed to last for more than one generation.

Prior to the passage of this law, it was possible in some circumstances to create a trust that would pass a life estate from successive generations in a family, limited only by the so-called rule against perpetuities. It is to be recalled that the rule against perpetuities does not permit the creation of any property right which lasts more than the duration of the life of an individual already in existence, plus an additional twenty-one years.

The new so-called generation-skipping transfer tax law imposes a tax on any trust which has beneficiaries in two or more succeeding generations that are younger than the creator or grantor of the trust. Stated another way, if three or more generations are involved, the tax applies.

For example, a trust created by a grandparent for the life of a son, with the property passing to the son's children on the son's death would be the type of trust that is subject to tax. In this case, the estate of the creator (grandparent) would be liable for the federal estate tax on the transfer to the son. In addition, the new generation-skipping transfer tax would be payable on the son's death. The transfer tax is computed as if the value of the trust property were added to the son's estate at the time of his death. In effect, this generation-skipping tax is designed as a substitute for the tax that the son's estate would have paid on that property if the grandparent had bequested the property to the son outright.

In contrast, another rather common type of trust is not subject to the generation-skipping transfer tax. This would be a trust created by one spouse for the benefit of the surviving spouse who holds a life estate, with the property eventually going to the children or other heirs at the time of the surviving spouse's death. For purposes of the law, the creator's spouse is always regarded as being in the same generation as the creator, regardless of the fact that the surviving spouse may be considerably younger or older than the creator. In this type of trust, only two generations are involved in the trust transfers. The difference that makes this trust exempt from the generation-skipping tax is in the number of generations affected in the transfers. There were only two generations, rather than the three generations in the example prior to this one.

If a grandparent sets up a trust, with the proceeds going directly to grandchildren, this trust would also not be subject to the so-called generation-skipping trust tax. Here again, only two generations would be involved. The basic test concerning whether a trust will be subjected to the generation-skipping transfer tax is dependent on the number of heirs of succeeding generations that benefit from the trust.

$250,000 EXCLUSION FOR EACH GRANDCHILD

The generation-skipping transfer tax law provides that a grandfather or grandmother may set up a trust, passing property to a child who has grandchildren. Upon the death of the child, property worth up to $250,000 for each child is exempt. Accordingly, a grandparent who set up a trust for eventual distribution to four grandchildren could exempt property worth $1 million by using this exclusion.

AVOIDING GENERATION-SKIPPING TRANSFER TAX

Some individuals may have an estate valued in excess of the total exclusions for grandchildren (the number of grandchildren × $250,000 each). In a situation of this kind, the generation-skipping transfer tax may be avoided by setting up separate trusts for children and grandchildren, rather than transferring the property through a three-tiered arrangement.

For purposes of this tax, generally a grandfather or grandmother is one generation, a son or daughter is a second generation, a grandson or granddaughter is a third generation and offspring of a grandson or a granddaughter is a fourth generation. In some situations, the dividing line from one generation to another is not completely clear. The *Federal Tax Reform Act of 1976,* Code Section 2611, defines generations, for purposes of the generation-skipping transfer law. This procedure for ascertaining generations is set out in Appendix 12.

A FINAL NOTE: OBTAIN ASSISTANCE WHEN YOU NEED IT!

It is not reflection on your ability to get outside assitance in protecting your estate and in planning methods to pass on your property. Most of us can use help in projects of this kind. This book, or any book, can only spread before you a representative view of some of problems and possibilities in estate protection.

Realizing the nature of these problems, you may work out your own devices, with professional help from time to time. There are few of us who have the over-all knowledge and ability to completely take over in place of lawyer, tax specialist, investment counselor, or trust advisor. This does not mean that you should immediately go out and hire experts in all those fields. But start by having a lawyer write a will that is appropriate to your current needs. Then, make additional plans and work toward financial independence, obtaining professional help when needed.

Yours for a carefree time in the coming years, and a pleasant contemplation of those things you may pass along to your heirs!

Glossary

Some words on this list have more than one legal usage. These additional meanings may be found in a comprehensive legal dictionary. The usages here are those that pertain to wills and trusts.

administrator. An individual designated by a probate court to settle the estate of an individual dying without a will.

ambulatory will. A phrase sometimes used in legal circles to denote the power which a testator (maker) of a will has to alter his or her will at any time.

ancillary administration. An estate settlement in a state where the deceased owned property, but which is a different state from that of the deceased's domicile, where the main estate is administered.

annual exclusion. The $3,000 exclusion from federal taxes permitted in any year on a gift from one person to another. The husband and wife may each use the $3,000 exclusion in one year, indefinitely.

annuity. A set amount of money, bequeathed, contracted for, or granted, payable at specified periods for a set time, or for life.

attestation. The act of witnessing a legal document, such as a will. The execution of the will is the signing by the testator (maker), while the attestation is the signing to bear witness to the maker's signature.

beneficiary. A person who inherits under the terms of a will, or an individual or organization for whose benefit a trust is set up.

bequest. A gift left by will. In modern times used interchangeably with the term legacy. A devise by will.

cestui que trust. The beneficiary of a trust.

charitable remainder trust. An agreement with a charity, whereby the charity pays income on the amount of the trust fund to one or more beneficiaries for life, with the remainder of the trust fund then belonging to the charity.

chancellor. A probate judge.

Clifford trust. A trust created to provide income for someone else, while retaining the principal for the creator, for the purpose of reducing income tax liability by the creator. A Clifford trust is sometimes called a short trust or reversionary trust. For tax purposes, a trust of this kind must run for at least ten years or until the earlier death of the donee. In a typical trust of this kind, the donor created the trust to give income to someone that the donor or grantor would normally support anyway, such as a dependent parent or in-law. Under this arrangement, the income tax on the income produced from the trust fund would be paid by the beneficiary of the trust, who is in a low income tax bracket and may not pay any tax at all. In the meantime, the donor, who is usually in a very high income bracket, is relieved of paying income tax on this income. At the termination of the trust, or on the death of the donee, the principal in the trust fund reverts back to the creator. Another typical situation where this kind of trust is used is to accumulate money for the education of a grandchild.

codicil. An addition to a will that changes, modifies, or explains the original will.

collaterals. Those relatives who are descended from a common ancestor, but who are not in the same line. Those relatives who are off to the side in the family tree. For example, an aunt or uncle would be a collateral, but a grandfather would not be. Collateral descendents are those not directly related as ascendants or descendents.

community property. The property ownership system used by a husband and wife in eight states: Arizona, California, Idaho, Louisiana, New Mexico, Nevada, Texas, and Washington, as well as Puerto Rico. The essential principle is that all property acquired during the marriage belongs equally to both, regardless of whose name it is in. Generally, to be separate property and not community property, the property or money used to buy the separate property must be kept separate from the time of marriage.

conformed copy. An exact copy of a will or other legal document which has had copies filled in by a written explanation of things that could not be copied. For example, the handwritten date and signature on a will could not be copied exactly, so the signature blank would be filled with a notation such as: "Signed by Barnaby Brown on October 5, 1979."

construction proceeding. A legal hearing to determine whether a written instrument qualifies or is operable as a will.

conjoint will. Another name for a joint will.

consanguinity. A relationship by blood, rather than by marriage.

constructive trust. A trust raised up by the courts in a situation where one individual gains title to the property of another, as through fraud or clerical error. The courts regard the owner as holding such property in trust for the individual who should have title (is entitled to beneficial enjoyment) of the property. This is not the type of trust that would be created in setting up an estate plan.

contingent beneficiary. A beneficiary who takes according to the terms of a will, but only if an uncertain specified condition or event has taken place.

corpus. The property or money that is given to the trustees for the founding of a trust. The res, the body of the trust or the principal.

counter will. Another name for a reciprocal will.

court of ordinary. Another name given to a probate court, court of orphans, or surrogate court in some areas. Whatever the name, these courts all have jurisdiction in the administration of estates and wills. Courts of ordinary were renamed in some states, such as New Jersey, South Carolina, and Texas.

court of orphans. A name used in some states for a court otherwise known as a probate court, surrogate court, or court of *ordinary*.

creator. The person who sets up a trust, providing the money or property that is the corpus or res (body) used to fund the trust. Also called a grantor, settlor, donor, or founder of the trust.

curtesy. A husband's right to all or part of his deceased wife's property. This right is now defined or set by state law, and the extent of the right varies from state to state where curtesy is recognized. Curtesy is an old right from English law.

decedent. A dead person; a deceased.

declaration of trust. A written instrument used to set up a trust. Sometimes called a trust indenture, or an indenture of trust. It places ownership of the property in the hands of the trustee, for the use and benefit of some other person (the cestui que trust, or beneficiary).

descent and distribution. A system for disbursing property by hereditary succession; a system of inheritance from parents or other relatives.

devise. A gift made by will. In modern times used interchangeably with bequest or legacy. To make a bequest by will.

distribution. The act of parceling out property from an estate to those entitled thereto by inheritance or by will.

donee. An individual to whom a gift is made.

donor. Any person who gives something to another. The maker of a will is a donor of money or property distributed under the provisions of the will. The person who places property in trust for the benefit of another is a donor of the trust.

double will. Another name for a reciprocal will. This type of will may also be called a mutual will, or counter will.

dower. The wife's automatic right in her deceased husband's real estate, assigned to her by operation of law in some states. The dower right was adopted from old English law in most states in the United States, and is now regulated by statute where the right still exists.

dry trust. A trust which merely vests or places the legal title in the trustee, not requiring any additional performance or activity on the trustee's part to carry out the trust.

election. The right to choose. For example, the right to elect between the amount granted in a will, or the statutory amount that state law may reserve as a minimum share of a husband's or wife's estate.

escheat. The reversion of ownership of property to the state, when there is no will and no legal heir can be found. A reversion.

estate. Everything an individual owns, including property over which that person exercises decisive control. This includes personal property such as clothing, furniture, jewelry, cars, etc., and real property such as land, buildings, or interest in real estate.

ex parte. On one side only, or with only one side represented. An ex parte order is one granted by a court at the request of one party to a judicial proceeding without notification to the other side involved.

execution. The act of completing a written instrument, such as a will or deed. The execution of a will requires the signing of the maker and witnesses in conformity with strict legal requirements. The execution of some other legal documents may require some different actions. For example, the execution of a deed requires a signature plus an actual delivery of the instrument to the person who is to take the property.

executor. A man appointed by the maker of a will to carry out the provisions of the will after the maker's death.

executrix. The female counterpart of an executor.

express trust. A trust declared or created in specific terms or language, almost always in writing. It is distinguished from a trust inferred by the courts from the conduct or dealings of the parties.

extremis. In one's last illness; on the deathbed.

fiduciary. An administrator, executor, or trustee.

founder. The person who sets up a trust. Also called a grantor, creator, settlor, or donor of a trust.

gift inter vivos. A gift made during the lifetime of the maker, and not by will. A gift made by verbal promise, followed by an acceptance by the donee (recipient of the gift). The gift becomes an absolute transfer, as distinguished from a will, which does not become effective until the death of the donor.

grantor. The creator of a trust, the individual who puts up the money, also called the creator, founder, settlor, or donor of the trust.

guardian. An individual appointed by a court to take care of another individual and/or that individual's property because that second person is incompetent or is under legal age.

heir. One who inherits from a deceased individual.

holographic will. A type of will that is completely written, signed, and dated in the handwriting of the maker. Witnesses are not required. Holographic wills are permitted by statute in approximately one-half the states in the United States. The formal requirements are that the entire will be handwritten, handdated, and signed by the maker without any deviation whatever.

implied trust. A trust created or implied by law to achieve justice between the parties. It is distinguished from an express trust, which is created by express language of the parties involved.

indenture of trust. Same as trust indenture or declaration of trust.

inter vivos trust. Sometimes called a living trust, since it goes into operation while the maker is still alive. It is distinguished from a testamentary trust, which goes into effect after the death of the individual who set up the trust arrangement.

intestate. Having died without a valid will.

irrevocable trust. A trust agreement which cannot be changed or revoked by the individual who set up the trust arrangement, except with the mutual approval of all the parties to the agreement and the beneficiaries of the trust.

issue. A direct descendent, such as a son or a grandaughter.

joint tenants with right of survivorship, or joint tenancy. An ownership arrangement for property, in which two or more individuals own jointly, with equal rights to share in its enjoyment during their lives, and with the survivor eventually receiving the entire property.

joint will. A single instrument that serves as a will for two or more individuals, usually a husband and wife, and is jointly signed by them. The instrument disposes of the makers' several interests in property owned by them in common, or of their separate property treated as a common fund being given to a third person or persons. A joint will has legal differences from a reciprocal will. It is seldom used today, since a joint will is relatively inflexible as a means of disposing of different parts of an estate.

legacy. A gift left by will. In modern times used interchangeably with bequest. A devise.

letters of administration. The written court authorization, permitting an individual to handle the distribution of an estate as administrator

letters testamentary. The probate court's authorization to a specific individual to serve as an executor or executrix of a will.

life estate. An estate held by a tenant for the duration of his or her life, or for the life of some other person or persons.

life income beneficiary. A beneficiary who is granted an income for life.

lineal descent. Descent in a family line, such as father and son, or mother and son.

living trust. See Inter Vivos Trust.

living will. A written request by an individual who does not want his or her life continued by artificial means or artificial support systems when there is no question that the individual will have no meaningful functions in the time that remains prior to death. A living will is a misnomer, since it is not a true will at all.

ministerial trust. A trust which requires no further exercise of reason or understanding than any intelligent person must necessarily use. A trust in which no discretion is needed on the part of the trustee.

mutual will. Another name for a reciprocal will.

mystic testament. A form of will used in the state of Louisiana, which is an outgrowth of old Spanish law, from the time when Louisiana belonged to Spain. It is a sealed instrument signed by the maker, presented closed and sealed to a notary and witnesses. There are other specific formal requirements under the Civil Code of Louisiana, article 1584.

naked trust. A trust which requires no action on the part of the trustee, beyond turning over money or property to the beneficiary (cestui que trust). Sometimes called a dry or passive trust.

non-intervention will. A type of will permitted in some states that allows the executor to handle the estate without putting up a bond guaranteeing the executor's performance, and to settle the estate without the detailed supervision or intervention of any court whatsoever. This permits the estate to be settled in less time and at less expense than if the will did not have this provision. The executor, in this type of will or in any other type, is liable to the heirs in a civil suit for embezzlement or mishandling of assets. This kind of will is usually an excellent arrangement for a person who leaves property to a spouse and children, with the spouse serving as executor. It is highly unlikely that the spouse would cheat himself or herself or the children.

nuncupative will. An oral will. This is a type of will that is not recognized in many states because of the possibility of fraud. It usually has restrictions and limitations regarding its use, even in those states where recognized.

olographic will. A spelling variation for a holographic will.

ordinary. A judicial officer in some states, who has statutory powers to handle matters relating to wills, probate, the administration of estates, and guardianships. The ordinary is the equivalent of the judge of probate in some states.

orphans' court. The name used in some states, such as Delaware, New Jersey, and Pennsylvania, for courts known as probate or surrogate courts in most other states.

passive trust. A trust in which the trustee has no active duty to perform, except that of turning over trust funds to the beneficiary.

per stirpes. A system for dividing an estate whereby shares are given equally by family groupings, and not given as so many individuals (per capita). Under per stirpes distribution, the two children of a testator would share equally from the testator. But if one of these children was deceased, leaving six children, each such grandchild of the testator would receive one-sixth of one-half, or one-twelfth of the total.

personal representative. Generally used to mean an executor, executrix, administrator, or administratrix of a deceased person. Occasionally used in the law of wills to mean heirs, next of kin, or descendants of the deceased.

precatory, precatory trust. Words of entreaty, or request, as may be used in a will. Sometimes words used in a will do not amount to a positive command or testamentary disposition; however a court will say that the law will infer or raise a trust from such words. This is called a *precatory trust.*

primogeniture. The first-born child. The out-dated rule of old English law that the eldest inherited everything from the parent. This rule was apparently followed to protect the estates of the great lords.

principal of the trust. The capital, corpus, res, or body of a trust, as distinguished from the interest or income from the capital.

pouring over, pour-over trust, pour-over will. Adding estate assets to a trust is called "pouring over." A will which disposes of trust monies or assets in this way is known as a *pour-over will.* A trust set up by a will that makes use of this pour-over idea is called a pour-over trust.

probate. The legal procedure by which state courts accept a will as authentic. This acceptance enables the executor to collect and pay debts, pay taxes, sell off property, distribute bequests, and perform the other responsibilities of settling an estate. A number of states have simplified their probate procedures, but the process is usually expensive and slow. Not all the property or items owned by the deceased go through probate. However, life insurance, payable to a beneficiary other than the estate, money or property left in trust, or bank accounts held in a joint tenancy arrangement are exempt from probate.

probate court. A court that handles probate matters, wills, administration of estates, and guardianship matters. Sometimes called a surrogate court, orphans court, or court of ordinary, depending on the state of location.

probate judge. A chancellor; a surrogate; the judge of a probate court, handling the distribution of estates. Such a judge may also handle guardianship matters, insanity hearings, and commitments.

reciprocal will. A will in which two or more persons make reciprocal or mutual provisions to dispose of property in favor of each other. A reciprocal will is also known as a mutual will, double will, or counter will. It is not the same as a joint will.

remainder. An interest in property which takes effect only after the expiration of a prior estate in the property. This prior estate is generally a life estate.

remainderman. The name given to an individual or organization which gets trust property after the trust has ended.

res. The capital or donative part of a trust that is the substance of the trust fund; the corpus. The res is distinguished from the interest which is the money earned on the res.

residuary estate. That part of an estate that is left over after specific bequests in a will have been satisfied.

resulting trust. A trust set up by operation of law, usually in a court of equity. It arises where the legal estate in property is transferred, conveyed, or disposed of, but the intent is inferred from the terms of the disposition. Or it may arise from the accompanying facts and circumstances, that the beneficial interest is not to go along with or be enjoyed along with the legal title.

reversionary trust. See Clifford Trust.

revocable trust. A trust that can be terminated or changed at the desire of the creator.

revocation. The voiding, or ending of a right, of a legal privilege, or of an instrument, such as a will.

rule against perpetuities. The legal principal that full ownership of property cannot be postponed longer than that of a life already in being, plus an additional twenty-one years. In other words, someone must receive a fee simple interest (outright ownership) within the lifetime of any living heir, plus an additional twenty-one years. This means that you cannot devise a series of life estates, one after the other, indefinitely.

self-proved will. A will, that in some states, is automatically accepted as valid unless contested in court. By statutory provision, this is a rebuttable presumption that the will is valid. This is usually a benefit for the heirs, since it eliminates the cost and time of obtaining witnesses who would testify to the preparation and signing of the will. This procedure is not uniformly permitted under state laws, however.

settlor. A person who owns property and places it in a trust. The settlor of a trust is also called the creator, donor, or founder of the trust.

short trust. See Clifford Trust.

spouse. A married person; husband or wife.

standby trust. A trust that is complete, but that as yet has not been given much funding.

subscribe. To write one's signature at the end of a written document or legal instrument. To subscribe may mean to execute a will as maker, or to sign as a witness to the will, or to be a subscribing witness.

surrogate court. Synonymous with probate court, orphans' court, or court of ordinary.

testament. A legal term that is identical with the terms will or last will and testament.

testamentary capacity. That measure of mental ability which is recognized by the courts as sufficient to permit one to make a will.

testamentary class. A group or body of persons, uncertain in number, but ascertainable at the time a will takes effect, with each person in the class taking equal or other definite portions under the will. For example, a devise to "each of my grandchildren" would be a devise to all individuals in that testamentary class.

testamentary disposition. A gift, or disposition of property by will.

testamentary trust. A trust established by will, going into effect when the creator dies.

testate. The condition of leaving a valid will when one dies.

testator. An individual who makes a will, or has it made. One who dies leaving a valid will.

Totten trust. The placing of money in a bank or savings account in your own name as trustee for someone else. It is not a real trust at all, since the creator can take back the money at any time. If the creator should die, the funds on deposit go to the beneficiary, and are not a part of the decedent's estate. In effect, it is a simple and convenient method for making tentative provision for limited objectives, such as education for a grandchild.

trust. Basically, a legal arrangement in which money or property is given to a new legal entity, called the trust. This money or property is to be administered by an individual or institution (such as a bank) called the trustee. A trust is administered for the best interests of a designated beneficiary. The creator may be the beneficiary, although it is usually another individual or an organization. The trustee who accepts the responsibility of administration is paid a fee, is required to account for all money or assets received, and is liable in a civil lawsuit for mishandling or for embezzlement. The beneficiary is entitled to receive the income or distribution of property, under the terms of the trust.

The essential requirements or elements of a trust are: (1) a designated beneficiary, (2) a designated trustee, (3) assets or property sufficiently identified to enable title to them to pass to the trustee (who is the technical owner, with the beneficiary said to be the beneficial owner), (4) and actual delivery to the trustee of the property or indicia of title, with the intention of passing ownership to the trust.

trust indenture. A trust agreement, generally called a declaration of trust or an indenture of trust.

trustor. One who creates a trust; a settlor; a creator; a founder; a donor of a trust.

unofficious will. A will that disregards some or all of the natural heirs, leaving property to those who are not the "natural objects of the testator's bounty."

usufruct. The right to use, occupy, and enjoy property, drawing all the profit, utility, or advantage that it will produce, provided this is done without harming or altering the substance or value of the property.

ward. An individual incapable of managing his or her own affairs, and for whom a court has appointed a guardian.

will. A legal instrument which is an expression or declaration of an individual's wishes concerning the disposition of property, to take effect immediately after death. When the term will is used, it commonly refers to a so-called formal will which must be executed before witnesses and under other specific conditions set out by state law. In addition to formal wills, holographic or nuncupative wills are of equal validity in some states. See holographic will; nuncupative will; mystic will (used in Louisiana only).

will contest. A legal dispute concerning whether there is or is not a valid will. This is a contest about whether an alleged will should be admitted to probate as being validly and actually made by the testator. A will contest is distinguished from a dispute about the validity or legality of individual bequests in the will (such as a situation where the maker disinherited his son in favor of a friendly hussy).

Appendixes

APPENDIX 1:
An Estate
Evaluation Form

Your estate cannot be precisely valued until after your death, when assets are appraised or sold. But you can make a good approximation of present worth by completing this form. Make estimates where necessary. It is also worth noting that estate values may increase considerably in future years.

	Estimated Value	*Spouse's Property*	*Joint Ownership*
Bank accounts (checking)	$ _____	$ _____	$_____
Checking accounts	_____	_____	_____
Government bonds	_____	_____	_____
Real estate	_____	_____	_____
Home equity	_____	_____	_____
Personal property:			
Furniture	_____	_____	_____
Cars	_____	_____	_____
Jewelry	_____	_____	_____
Antiques	_____	_____	_____
Art	_____	_____	_____
Second home	_____	_____	_____
Other	_____	_____	_____
Life insurance	_____	_____	_____
Group policies	_____	_____	_____
Pension plan benefits	_____	_____	_____
Profit Sharing	_____	_____	_____
Equity in a business	_____	_____	_____
Money owed to you	_____	_____	_____
Totals	$ _____	$ _____	$_____
Less loans owed, except those covered by credit life insurance	$ _____	$ _____	$_____
Total Estate Value	$ _____		

APPENDIX 2:
Things to Do Immediately After the Death of Loved One or Friend

The following suggestions may be used as a checkoff list to be followed automatically in time of grief:

1. Notify the authorities—usually the police or coroner, if the death was unexpected and a doctor was not in attendance. Even if the death was from natural causes, all states require a doctor, coroner, or medical examiner to examine the body.

2. Call a mortician to take over the body.

3. Ascertain whether the deceased had any wishes about giving away organs, corneas from the eyes, or other body parts as gifts or transplants. Gifts of this kind may be unusable if there is much delay.

4. Arrange to obtain copies of the death certificiate from the mortician or attending doctor. These are frequently needed to document survivor benefits, insurance, and other paperwork.

5. Make arrangements for a burial lot or plot, unless the deceased or the deceased's spouse already owns a lot with space.

6. Inform relatives and kin, along with friends.

7. Work out funeral arrangements for burial, cremation, or an appropriate arrangement.

8. Gather up any documents that may be related to the deceased's business affairs, tax matters, property concerns, personal papers, and so on. Furnish originals or copy to the executor, if known.

9. Furnish the deceased's will to the executor or executrix.

APPENDIX 3:
Typical Will Form—
Available in
Stationery Stores

LAST WILL & TESTAMENT

I,..., a resident of

...., California,

declare this to be my last Will and revoke all other Wills previously

made by me:

First:

.........: I appoint...

....

as Execut........of this Will...

....

....

This will was signed by me on the........day of ...., 19.....,

at ...., California.

....

The Foregoing Instrument was, on the date thereof, signed by the

test ....,

...., in our presence,

we being present at the same time, and.....he then declared to us that

the said instrument was h........ last Will; and we, at the request of

said ....,

and in h.........presence, and in the presence of each other, have signed

the same as witnesses. We further declare that at the time of signing this will the said ....

appeared to be of sound and disposing mind and memory and not

acting under duress, menace, fraud or the undue influence of any

person whomsoever.

....residing at ....
<small>Signature of Witness</small>

....residing at ....
<small>Signature of Witness</small>

....residing at ....
<small>Signature of Witness</small>

APPENDIX 4:
Anatomical
Gift Donor Card

If you intend to make a gift of body organs at the time of your death, this may be authorized by attaching a signed, witnessed card to the back of your driver's license. A typical card of this kind is as follows:

Pursuant to the Uniform Anatomical Gift Act, I hereby give, effective upon my death:

A_____Any needed organ or parts

B_____Parts or organs listed _____

_____
Date

_____

_____
Signature of Donor

_____
Witness

_____
Witness   DL-290 (NEW 7/76)

APPENDIX 5:
A Typical Living Will

(Place)

, _____

_____
(Date)

To My Doctor, Members of My
Family, and Legal Authorities:

This is a statement of my desires, whatever the future holds. It was written while in good health and in full realization that we can never predict physical infirmities or problems that may arise in coming years.

I do not want to be kept alive when survival can only be continued by mechanical life-support systems and artificial means. I want to be permitted to die in dignity, if additional life will be meaningless.

Should I be beyond recovery, I request that whatever drugs are necessary be used to prevent suffering at the time of my death.

_____

APPENDIX 6:
A Typical Probate of Will Check Sheet

Estate of   Case No.

Date of Death   Date of Hearing

Prepare photographic copies of Will (at least 2).

If will is Holographic, also prepare a typed copy for use with Petition.
File the Original Will.

File Petition for Probate of Will in duplicate. Designate the Daily Journal or California Newspaper Service Bureau paper for "publication".

Prepare, complete and as early as possible prior to date of hearing file evidence of Subscribing Witness or Affidavit of Holographic Will, with photographic copy of Will attached. (Signatures of both the Witness and the attorney are required.)

Note: Notices to Heirs will be mailed, publication re Notice of Hearing will be completed, and Affidavits and Proofs thereof will be filed and conformed copies mailed to you by our paper.

Note: In branch courts, Notes of Probate Attorneys are mailed to you.

After the Hearing: Prepare (1) Order Admitting Will to Probate and (2) Letters Testamentary or Letters of Administration with Will Annexed (C.T.A.). Submit them for approval by the Probate Attorney. (In Central District only, the County Clerk will prepare Orders, Cost $10.)

Bond, if needed: Amount _____

Submit with Order and Letters. _____

Letters issued on _____

Request appointment of Referee: (Necessary only in Central District)

Name of Referee _____

Address _____

Phone _____

Notice to Creditors _____

Date of First publication _____

The Daily Journal/Bureau will publish this notice automatically when Letters are issued. Following publication, proof will be filed and a copy mailed to attorney.

File inventory and Appraisement in duplicate.

Family Allowance: File Petition, if necessary. Order granted _____

Sale of Real Property: _____

Date of Sale _____

On request, the Daily Journal/Bureau will publish this notice. Forms
are supplied. You will be notified re date of sale.

Appraisal of Real Property to be sold must be within 12 months
of date of sale.

Return of Sale of Real Property: Prepare and file. Hearing date is

Prepare and submit Order Confirming Sale for approval by Probate
Attorney.

Obtain Certified Copy of Order Confirming Sale and Record in the
County where property is located.

County _____

Date recorded _____

Execute Deed: Date _____

Petitions to Borrow Money, To Mortgate, To Execute Deed of Trust,
To Lease, or To Convey. File in duplicate. Designate newspaper
for publication. _____

The Daily Journal/Bureau will prepare and publish or post the proper
notice; proof is filed and a copy mailed to attorney.

Claims: Have all claims been filed? _____ Are they Paid? __

Final Acount and Petition for Distribution filed on Date of Hearing __

Taxed Paid:

   (1) State Inheritance Tax_____ Receipt filed ____

   (2) State Income Tax _____ Receipt filed ____

   (3) Federal Estate Tax_____ Receipt filed ____

   (4) Federal Income Tax _____ Receipt filed ____

Decree of Distribution signed by Judge _____ Date _____

   Certified copies ordered _____

Legacies and heirs paid _____

Receipts filed _____

If Real Property is involved, as Certified Copy of Decree of Distribution been Recorded?

   County _____

Date_____

Final Discharge filed _____

Form courtesy of: THE LOS ANGELES DAILY JOURNAL, 210
South Spring St., Los Angeles, Calif. 90012, Telephone: 625-2141

APPENDIX 7:
Credit for State
Death Taxes

(b) Amount of Credit.—The credit allowed by this section shall not exceed the appropriate amount stated in the following table:

If the adjusted taxable estate is:	*The maximum tax credit shall be:*
Not over $90,000	8/10ths of 1% of the amount by which the adjusted estate exceeds $40,000.
Over $90,000 but not over $140,000	$400 plus 1.6% of the excess over $90,000
Over $140,000 but not over $240,000	$1,200 plus 2.4% of the excess over $140,000.
Over $240,000 but not over $440,000	$3,600 plus 3.2% of the excess over $240,000.
Over $440,000 but not over $640,000	$10,000 plus 4% of the excess over $440,000.
Over $640,000 but not over $840,000	$18,000 plus 4.8% of the excess over $640,000.
Over $840,000 but not over $1,040,000	$27,600 plus 5.6% of the excess over $840,000.
Over $1,040,000 but not over $1,540,000	$38,800 plus 6.4% of the excess over $1,040,000.
Over $1,540,000 but not over $2,040,000	$70,800 plus 7.2% of the excess over $1,540,000.
Over $2,040,000 but not over $2,540,000	$106,800 plus 8% of the excess over $2,040,000.
Over $2,540,000 but not over $3,040,000	$146,800 plus 8.8% of the excess over $2,540,000.

Over $3,040,000 but not
over $3,540,000 ....$190,800 plus 9.6% of the
excess over $3,040,000.

Over $3,540,000 but not
over $4,040,000 ....$238,800 plus 10.4% of the
excess over $3,540,000.

Over $4,040,000 but not
over $5,040,000 ....$290,800 plus 11.2% of the
excess over $4,040,000.

Over $5,040,000 but not
over $6,040,000 ....$402.800 plus 12% of the
excess over $5,040,000.

Over $6,040,000 but not
over $7,040,000 ....$522,800 plus 12.8% of the
excess over $6,040,000.

Over $7,040,000 but not
over $8,040,000 ....$650,800 plus 13.6% of the
excess over $7,040,000.

Over $8,040,000 but not
over $9,040,000 ....$786,800 plus 14.4% of the
excess over $8,040,000.

Over $9,040,000 but not
over $10,040,000 ....$930,800 plus 15.2% of the
excess over $9,040,000.

Over $10,040,000..................$1,082,800 plus 16% of the
excess over $10,040,000.

APPENDIX 8:
Typical Power of Attorney Form

Because of the unlimited power that may be conferred by a Power of Attorney form, the authorization should never be given unless you trust the person on whom the power is conferred.

RECORDING REQUESTED BY

WHEN RECORDED MAIL TO

Name
Street
Address
City &
State
(SPACE ABOVE THIS LINE FOR RECORDER'S USE)_____

POWER OF ATTORNEY
GENERAL

Know All Men by These Presents: That I_____
_____

THE UNDERSIGNED (jointly and severally, if more than one) hereby make, constitute and appoint _____
_____,
my true and lawful Attorney for me and in my name, place and stead and for my use and benefit:

(a) To ask, demand, sue for, recover, collect and receive each and every sum of money, debt, account, legacy, bequest, interest, dividend, annuity and demand (which now is or hereafter shall become due, owing or payable) belonging to or claimed by me, and to use and take any lawful means for the recovery thereof by legal process or otherwise, and to execute and deliver a satisfaction or release therefor, together with the right and power to compromise or compound any claim or demand;

(b) To exercise any or all of the following powers as to real property, any interest therein and/or any building thereon: To contract for, purchase, receive and take possession thereof and of evidence of title thereto; to lease the same for any term or purpose, including leases for business, residence, and oil and/or mineral development; to sell, exchange, grant or convey the same with or without warranty; and to mortgage, transfer in trust, or otherwise encumber or hypothecate the same to secure payment of a negotiable or non-negotiable note or performance of any obligation or agreement;

(c) to exercise any or all of the following powers as to all kinds of personal property and goods, wares and merchandise, choses in action and other property in possession or in action: to contract for, buy, sell, exchange, transfer and in any legal manner deal in and with the same; and to mortgage, transfer in trust, or otherwise encumber or hypothecate the same to secure payment of a negotiable or non-negotiable note or performance of any obligation or agreement;

(d) To borrow money and to execute and deliver negotiable or non-negotiable notes therefor with or without security; and to loan money and receive negotiable or non-negotiable notes therefor with such security as he shall deem proper;

(e) To create, amend, supplement and terminate any trust and to instruct and advise the trustee of any trust wherein I am or may be trustor or beneficiary; to represent and vote stock, exercise stock rights, accept and deal with any dividend, distribution or bonus, join in any corporate financing, reorganization, merger, liquidation, consolidation or other action and the extension, compromise, conversion, adjustment, enforcement or foreclosure, singly or in conjunction with others of any corporate stock, bond, note, debenture or other security; to compound, compromise, adjust, settle and satisfy any obligation, secured or unsecured, owing by or to me and to give or accept any property and/or money whether or not equal to or less in value than the amount owing in payment, settlement or satisfaction thereof;

(f) To transact business of any kind or class and as my act and deed to sign, execute, acknowledge and deliver any deed, lease, assignment of lease, covenant, indenture, indemnity, agreement, mortgage, deed of trust, assignment of mortgage or of the beneficial interest under deed of trust, extension or renewal of any obligation, subordination or waiver of priority, hypothecation, bottomry, charter-party, bill of lading, bill of sale, bill, bond, note, whether negotiable or non-negotiable, receipt, evidence of debt, full or partial release or satisfaction of mortgage, judgment and other debt, request for partial or full reconveyance of deed of trust and such other instruments in writing of any kind or class as may be necessary or proper in the premises.

Giving and Granting unto my said Attorney full power and authority to do and perform all and every act and thing whatsoever requisite, necessary or appropriate to be done in and about the premises as fully to all intents and purposes as I might or could do if personally present, hereby ratifying all that my said Attorney shall lawfully do or cause to be done by virtue of these presents. The powers and authority hereby conferred upon my said Attorney shall be applicable to all real and personal property or interests therein now owned or hereafter acquired by me and wherever situate.

My said Attorney is empowered hereby to determine in his sole discretion the time when, purpose for and manner in which any power herein conferred upon him shall be exercised, and the conditions, provisions and covenants of any instrument or document which may be executed by him pursuant hereto; and in the acquisition or disposition of real or personal property, my said Attorney shall have exclusive power to fix the terms thereof for cash, credit and/or property, and if on credit with or without security.

The undersigned, if a married woman, hereby further authorizes and empowers my said Attorney, as my duly authorized agent, to join in my behalf, in the execution of any instrument by which any community real property or any interest therein, now owned or hereafter acquired by my spouse and myself, or either of us, is sold, leased, encumbered, or conveyed.

When the context so requires, the masculine gender includes the feminine and/or neuter, and the singular number includes the plural.

WITNESS my hand this_____day of _____, 19_____

State of California,   }

                   }   SS.

    County of   }

On _____, before me, the undersigned, a Notary Public in and for said State, personally appeared ————————————————

————————————————————————————————

know to me to be the person————— whose
name——————————subscribed to the within instrument and ac-
knowledged that——————
executed the same.
                (Seal)————————————————————
Witness my hand and official seal. Notary Public in and for said
State.

POWER OF ATTORNEY—GENERAL
Wolcotts Form 1400—Rev. 10-62

> This standard form covers most usual problems
> in the field indicated. Before you sign, read it,
> fill in all blanks, and make changes proper to
> your transaction. Consult a lawyer if you doubt
> the form's fitness for your purpose.

APPENDIX 9:
Rates of Combined Federal Gift and Estate Taxes

This is the *Tax Reform Act of 1976,* enacted into law October 4, 1976, Public law 94–455, Code Section 2001:

IMPOSITION & RATE OF TAX

(a) **Imposition.**—A tax is hereby imposed on the transfer of the taxable estate of every decedent who is a citizen or resident of the United States.

(b) **Computation of Tax.**—The tax imposed by this section shall be the amount equal to the excess (if any) of—

    (1) a tentative tax computed in accordance with the rate schedule set forth in subsection (c) on the sum of—

        (A) the amount of the taxable estate, and
        (B) the amount of the adjusted taxable gifts, over

    (2) the aggregate amount of tax payable under chapter 12 with respect to gifts made by the decedent after December 31, 1976.

For purposes of paragraph (1) (B), the term 'adjusted taxable gifts' means the total amount of the taxable gifts (within the meaning of section 2503) made by the decedent after December 31, 1976, other than gifts which are includible in the gross estate of the decedent.

(c) Rate Schedule.—

If the amount with
respect to which the
tentative tax to be
computed is: *The tentative tax is:*

Not over $10,000 ....18 percent of such amount.
Over $10,000 but not
over $20,000.................$1,800, plus 20 percent of the excess
                                      of such amount over $10,000.
Over $20,000 but not
over $40,000.................$3,8000, plus 22 percent of the excess
                                      of such amount over $20,000.
Over $40,000 but not
over $60,000.................$8,200 plus 24 percent of the excess
                                      of such amount over $40,000.
Over $60,000 but not
over $80,000.................$13,000, plus 26 percent of the excess
                                      of such amount over $60,000.
Over $80,000 but not
over $100,000 ....$18,200, plus 28 percent of the excess
                                      of such amount over $80,000.
Over $100,000 but not
over $150,000 ....$23,800, plus 30 percent of the excess
                                      of such amount over $100,000.
Over $150,000 but not
over $250,000 ....$38,800, plus 32 percent of the excess
                                      of such amount over $150,000.
Over $250,000 but not
over $500,000 ....$70,800, plus 34 percent of the excess
                                      of such amount over $250,000.
Over $500,000 but not
over $750,000 ....$155,800, plus 37 percent of the excess
                                      of such amount over $500,000.
Over $750,000 but not
over $1,000,000.............$248,300, plus 39 percent of the excess
                                      of such amount over $750,000.
Over $1,000,000 but not
over $1,250,000.............$345,800, plus 41 percent of the excess
                                      of such amount over $1,000,000.
Over $1,250,000 but not
over $1,500,000.............$448,300, plus 43 percent of the excess
                                      of such amount over $1,250,000.

Over $1,500,000 but not
over $2,000,000.............$555,800, plus 45 percent of the excess
of such amount over $1,500,000.

Over $2,000,000 but not
over $2,500,000.............$780,800, plus 49 percent of the excess
of such amount over $2,000,000.

Over $2,500,000 but not
over $3,000,000.............$1,025,800, plus 53 percent of the excess of such amount over $2,500,000.

Over $3,000,000 but not
over $3,500,000.............$1,290,800, plus 57 percent of the excess of such amount over $3,000,000.

Over $3,500,000 but not
over $4,000,000.............$1,575,800, plus 61 percent of the excess of such amount over $3,500,000.

Over $4,000,000 but not
over $4,500,000.............$1,880,800, plus 65 percent of the excess of such amount over $4,000,000.

Over $4,500,000 but not
over $5,000,000.............$2,205,800, plus 69 percent of the excess of such amount over $4,500,000.

Over $5,000,000.............$2,550,800, plus 70 percent of the excess of such amount over $5,000,000.

APPENDIX 10:
Living Revocable Trust Incorporated Into "Pour-Over" Type Will

I, ___(name)___ , of ___(place)___ , State of _____ , hereby make this my last will, revoking all other wills previously made by me.

ARTICLE 1. I hereby appoint my wife, _____ , Executrix of this will and Trustee of my estate, requesting that no bond be required of her in either capacity. In the event of the disqualification, default, removal, or resignation of my wife, I hereby authorize my wife to appoint a successor Executor or Executrix of this will and Trustee of my estate, and to require or not to require as my wife sees fit, the execution of a bond. In the event of the failure of my wife to exercise this power of appointment, and in the event of the death, disqualification, default, removal, or resignation of the appointee, I appoint my (son, brother, etc.), _____ , executor of this will and Trustee of my estate, requesting that no bond be required of (him or her) as such. In the event of the default, disqualification, removal or resignation of my (son, brother, etc.) as executor, I appoint the (bank or trust company) or (place), (state) as Executor of this will and Trustee of my estate. When the word "Executor" is used in this will it shall be deemed to refer to either my executor or executrix, according to whichever shall be serving.

ARTICLE 2. This will and the (creator's name) Living Revocable Trust hereinafter referred to shall be construed as if the two instruments constituted a single document.

ARTICLE 3. My executor is instructed to pay all my just debts and funeral expenses, and to pay out of my residuary estate all estate taxes, inheritance taxes, transfer and succession taxes on the bequests and legacies given herein. My executor shall make no charges or claims against anyone receiving any money or property under the terms of this will, on account of such taxes as may be assessed because of such legacies or bequests.

ARTICLE 4. I hereby confirm and declare that all home furnishings, household items, furniture, equipment, and decorations of any kind utilized by my wife and me in our home belong to and shall remain the sole and exclusive property of my wife.

ARTICLE 5. If the order of our deaths cannot be determined, my wife, _____, shall be presumed to have survived me. This will is to be construed and administered upon that assumption and basis.

ARTICLE 6. All of my personal effects, correspondence, papers, clothing, and jewelry shall be given to my wife if she is living on the date of my death.

ARTICLE 7. All of my life insurance policies are to be paid to my testamentary trustee, thereby exempting these proceeds from state inheritance taxes, if legally possible.

ARTICLE 8. I specifically withhold exercising any power of appointment which I have under any trust agreement, contract, profit sharing arrangement, or will. Therefore, I bequeath and devise all my other property of any kind, personal, real, or mixed, in which I presently have, or my estate shall acquire an interest, present or future, contingent or vested, and excluding interests only where I have a legal right to appoint, to the acting trustee under the __(name)__ Living Revocable Trust executed by me on __(date) to be held and administered by the Trustee according to the instructions and terms thereof as set out in said instrument of Living Revocable Trust, as may be amended from time to time.

ARTICLE 9. I hereby empower my Executor, or any successor Executor, my Trustee, and any successor Trustee to have, utilize, and enjoy all of the powers granted to my Trustee under the __(name)__ Living Revocable Trust. and without limitation thereon the following additional express authority and powers:

(a) To receive loans to and make sales of property to and from the __(name)__ Living Revocable Trust, even though the individual serving as Trustee shall be the same individual serving as the fiduciary under this last will and testament.

(b) To file any necessary tax returns, separately or with my wife for the time prior to my death; to pay all or any part of the taxes that may be due, along with penalties or interest, in the sole discretion of my wife.

(c) To do every act and conduct any business that the Executor would have the right to do, if the Executor should be the individual owner thereof. The Executor shall conduct any business considered to be in the best interests of the beneficiaries of my estate. This includes the right to borrow, contract with respect to, collect, deal with, sue, invest, pledge, protect, allot, assign, enter into, exchange, mortgage, sell or otherwise dispose of, manage, insure, improve, hold, take possession of, repair, defend against suit, repair, rent, release, accept or exercise options, or do any other act for the benefit of the beneficiaries of my estate. In any eventuality, this grant of power is to be construed as including any and all powers granted to my Trustee in said __(name)__ Living Revocable Trust, and shall not be restricted in any way by the grant of specific powers named herein.

(d) To make any election permitted under the U.S. Internal Revenue Code that may be considered desirable by my Executor.

ARTICLE 10. If for any reason a court of competent jurisdiction shall declare this testamentary transfer invalid, or if for any reason the said __(name)__ Living Revocable Trust shall not be in existence at the time of my death, I hereby instruct that the estate disposed of by this will shall be managed, held, invested, and reinvested in exactly the same manner set forth in the said instrument of Living Revocable Trust, beginning with the date of my death, giving effect to all then existing amendments to said trust, if it shall be legal so to do, but in any event, giving effect to said trust as now in effect by the same Trustee therein named and defined who are to serve hereunder without the need to furnish sureties on their bonds, and for that purpose I do hereby incorporate that same instrument of Living Revocable Trust by reference into this my last will and testament. I also declare that said Living Revocable Trust was signed by me, not only before a notary public, but before __(one, two, or three)__witnesses as required by state law, and before which witnesses I executed said Living Revocable Trust, as if it constituted a last will and testament, so that this instrument can, in effect, be construed as a codicil to said __(name)__Living Revocable Trust.

ARTICLE 11. I declare that my Executor shall not be required to make any settlement with any court, or file any appraisal. In lieu thereof, within three months of each fiscal year of the administration of my estate, the Executor shall furnish a written account of the administration thereof to the current income beneficiaries. The signed approval of such accounting report shall be final and finding on all beneficiaries and each guardian of minor beneficiaries or those beneficiaries otherwise incompetent. The failure of any beneficiary to object in writing to the acting fiduciary to such an account within ninety days (90) after receipt of the same shall be final and binding to the same extent as if written approval were given as hereinbefore provided.

ARTICLE 12. All the property in my estate shall be finally distributed not later than twenty years and eleven months after the death of the last survivor of the group made up of my wife and my descendents living at the time of my death. This distribution shall be completed within the time herein specified, notwithstanding any provision of the __(name)__ Living Revocable Trust or any provision of this will, and at the expiration of such period if any portion of my estate remains undistributed, the same shall immediately vest in and be distributed to the individuals then entitled to receive income from the trust estate in the proportions to which they are entitled.

I, __(name)__ , a resident of __(town)__ , state of _____ , being in good health of mind and body, and being of a disposing mind and not acting under duress, fraud, menace, or the undue influence of any person whatever, hereby publish, make and declare this to be my last will and testament, expressly revoking all other and former wills and codicils to wills heretofore prepared or signed by me.

This will was signed by me on the _____ day of _____ , 19 ___ , at _____

The foregoing instrument, consisting of this and _____ prior pages, was, on the date thereof, signed by the __(testator, testatrix)__ , in our presence, we being present at the same time, and __(he, she)__ then declared to us that the said instrument was __(his, her)__ last will and testament; and we, at the request of __(testator)__ , and in __(his, her)__ presence, and in the presence of each other, have signed the same as witnesses. We further declare that at the time of signing this will the said __ (testator) __appeared to be of sound and disposing mind and memory, and not acting under duress, menace, fraud, or the undue influence of any person whatever.

__(signature of witness)__ residing at _____
__(signature of witness)__ residing at _____
__(signature of witness)__ residing at _____

APPENDIX 11:
Credits Allowed on Federal Estate Tax, to Avoid Double Taxation of Successive Estates Where Short Time Intervenes

Section 2013 of the U.S. Internal Revenue Code of 1954 provides some relief against double taxation of assets that were taxed as part of the estate of another decedent within the prior ten years:

Number of Years Ago When Prior Decedent Died	Percentage Credit Allowed for Prior Tax Payment
2 years	100%
3 to 4 years	80%
5 to 6 years	60%
7 to 8 years	40%
9 to 10 years	20%

This credit is limited, however, to the amount of the second estate that is attributable to specific assets that were taxed in the first estate. Several authorities consider the application of this code section as among the most confusing and complicated in the field of estate tax law.

APPENDIX 12:
How Specific Generations
Are Identified
or Distinguished in a
Generation-Skipping Trust

The *Tax Reform Act of 1976* (public law 94-455, passed October 4, 1976) specified rules for identifying or distinguishing generations in a generation-skipping trust. While this law limited the advantages that had previously been ejoyed by this type of trust, the law was specific concerning the identification of generations. Code provisions are as follows:

CODE SEC. 2611. GENERATION-SKIPPING TRANSFER.

(a) **Generation-Skipping Transfer Defined.**—For purposes of this chapter, the terms "generation-skipping transfer" and "transfer" mean any taxable distribution or taxable termination with respect to a generation-skipping trust or trust equivalent.

(b) **Generation-Skipping Trust.**—For purposes of this chapter, the term "generation-skipping trust" means any trust having younger generation beneficiaries (within the meaning of section 2613(c)(1)) who are assigned to more than one generation.

(c) **Ascertainment of Generation.**—For purposes of this chapter, the generation to which any person (other than the grantor) belongs shall be determined in accordance with the following rules:

(1) an individual who is a lineal descendant of a grandparent of the grantor shall be assigned to that generation which results from comparing the number of generations be-

tween the grandparent and such individual with the number of generations between the grandparent and the grantor,

(2) an individual who has been at any time married to a person described in paragraph (1) shall be assigned to the generation of the person so described and an individual who has been at any time married to the grantor shall be assigned to the grantor's generation,

(3) a relationship by the half blood shall be treated as a relationship by the whole blood,

(4) a relationship by legal adoption shall be treated as a relationship by blood,

(5) an individual who is not assigned to a generation by reason of the foregoing paragraphs shall be assigned to a generation on the basis of the date of such individual's birth, with—

   (A) an individual born not more than 12½ years after the date of the birth of the grantor assigned to the grantor's generation,

   (B) an individual born more than 12½ years but not more than 37½ years after the date of the birth of the grantor assigned to the first generation younger than the grantor, and

   (C) similar rules for a new generation every 25 years,

(6) an individual who, but for this paragraph, would be assigned to more than one generation shall be assigned to the youngest such generation, and

(7) if any beneficiary of the trust is an estate or a trust, partnership, corporation, or other entity (other than an organization described in section 511(a)(2) and other than a charitable trust described in section 511(b)(2)),

each individual having an indirect interest or power in the trust through such entity shall be treated as a beneficiary of the trust and shall be assigned to a generation under the foregoing provisions of this subsection.

(d) **Generation-Skipping Trust Equivalent.**—

(1) **In general.**—For purposes of this chapter, the term "generation-skipping trust equivalent" means any arrangement which, although not a trust, has substantially the same effect as a generation-skipping trust.

(2) **Examples of arrangements to which subsection relates.**—Arrangements to be taken into account for purposes of determining whether or not paragraph (1) applies include (but are not limited to) arrangements involving life estates and remainders, estates for years, insurance and annuities, and split interests.

(3) **References to trust include references to trust equivalents.**—Any reference in this chapter in respect of a generation-skipping trust shall include the appropriate reference in respect of a generation-skipping trust equivalent.

Index